REMEMBERING SYLHET

REMEMBERING SYLHET

Hindu and Muslim Voices from a Nearly Forgotten Story of India's Partition

ANINDITA DASGUPTA

MANOHAR
2014

First Published 2014

ISBN 978-81-7304-984-2

Published by
Ajay Jain *for*
Manohar Publishers & Distributors
4753/23 Ansari Road, Daryaganj
New Delhi 110002

Printed by
Salasar Imaging Systems
Delhi 110035

To

my father and my son

linking the past to the future

The identities of all respondents have been changed unless specifically permitted to use the real names. Any similarities, therefore, are purely coincidental.

Contents

Acknowledgements

At the very outset, I would like to express my sincere gratitude to SEPHIS, International Institute of Social History, the Netherlands, for supporting this study with a post-doctoral grant. I am grateful to Dr Ulbe Bosma, former co-ordinator of SEPHIS, Dr Marina de Regt, the present co-ordinator of SEPHIS and Ms Jacqueline Rutte, SEPHIS office manager, for their unfailing support, encouragement and patience throughout the grant period.

This work owes a great deal to Professor Willem Van Schendel whose writings on Partition refugees were a fertile source of ideas for this book. Professor Tanka Subba of the North East Hill University patiently read through every single draft and provided valuable comments and criticism. I was also fortunate to come into personal contact with some of the scholars widely cited in this study: Professors Amalendu Guha, Sujit Chaudhuri, Sanjib Baruah and Bidyut Chakrabarty. From each of them, I learnt valuable ways in which to understand and analyse the very complex history of Assam. My earliest academic inroads into memories of Sylhet Partition were made about ten years back in the course of a University Grants Commission (UGC) grant. Some of those initial ideas have also found their way into the present work.

Without the very able fieldwork support of Khaleda Sultana (then of the OKD Institute of Social Change and Economic Development, Guwahati) this study would not have been successfully completed. I am also deeply grateful to all the respondents, including my extended family and friends, who generously shared with me their life stories and memories of Partition. Dr Mihir Kumar Datta was kind enough to send me some important source material all the way from the United States. Carey L. Biron, Desk Editor at *Himal Southasian*, carefully copy-edited this book and added more grace and readability than it otherwise might have had. My friends Dr Reinier Bouwmeester, Rey Buono, Dr Lopita Nath, Neeta Singh and Chandrareka humored and supported me throughout the writing/publishing process. I am deeply grateful to Jishnu Baruah, IAS and Assam State Archives for giving me the permission to reprint the map of undivided India in this volume. To Mr Ramesh Jain and the editorial team at Manohar, New Delhi, I owe a special debt for publishing this book quickly.

My mother, not being of Sylhet origin herself and rather amused by my compulsive fascination for Sylhet, never failed to read my successive drafts and offer suggestions. As for my brother Arijit Dasgupta of *The Telegraph*, Kolkata, and all our Sylheti cousins, this book is as much their legacy, as mine. Santhirapalan, as always, allowed me all the time and space to pursue my ancestors and my 'imagined' homeland to my heart's content! My little Ishaan was conceived almost at the same time as this study. I hope someday he will discover his ancestors in the pages of this book.

An article titled 'Remembering Sylhet: A Forgotten Story of India's 1947 Partition' based on this research was published in the *Economic and Political Weekly* (2 August 2008). Another short article based on this research was published in *Himal Southasian* (14 August 2012). I thank all the readers who generously shared with me their ideas and resources on the Sylheti past through e-mails and letters to editors.

Finally, my gratitude to my father Dr Pradipta Kumar Dasgupta, from whose memories of Sylhet this work was born. My biggest regret is that he did not live to see its publication. It would have meant the world to him!

ANINDITA DASGUPTA

Introduction

This book presents new material on India's Partition of 1947 by telling the nearly forgotten story of the district of Sylhet (in colonial Assam) which was partitioned and ceded—barring a small Hindu pocket—to East Pakistan following the result of a referendum held on 6 and 7 July 1947. Partition, the break up of colonial India in 1947, has been the subject of substantial research in recent times, but has mostly focused on the two best-known cases—the Punjab and Bengal. This book represents one of the first attempts to document an account of the Sylhet Referendum and Partition based on interviews with eyewitnesses and integrate it to the growing corpus of India's Partition historiography.

Barely six weeks before India's Independence when the political big-wigs of the Indian National Congress and Muslim League were engaged in conversations and compromises regarding the imminent partition of Punjab and Bengal, in a quiet north-eastern corner of India—Sylhet district in Assam--unknown to most people, Hindus and Muslims were braving the incessant rains and water-logged fields, and streaming into make-shift poll booths to cast their life-changing votes to decide for themselves if their district would remain with India or join East Pakistan. A little over a month earlier, on 3 June, Lord Louis Mountbatten, the last viceroy of India, had proposed that a referendum be held in order that the people of Sylhet (a Muslim-majority district in the Hindu-majority province of Assam) could decide whether to stay in India or join Pakistan after Independence. Using eyewitness narratives, this book reconstructs the momentous Sylhet Referendum held on 6-7 July 1947 in which the people of Sylhet, or Sylhetis, cast votes to decide if the district would join India or Pakistan after Partition. Upon examination of the oral narratives, it becomes clear that both Sylheti Hindus and Muslims had contradictory expectations from the Referendum, and that neither community had correctly anticipated nor were emotionally, financially or physically prepared to deal with the unexpectedly contrary outcome of Partition. While it was widely hoped that the referendum would lead to a considered, unanimous and clear decision on the issue of Partition, the inescapable vivisection of Sylhet based on considerations of religious composition and geography, however, led to confusion, disappointment and large-scale displacement for both Hindus and Muslims instead. Such forced displacement of Sylhetis, the book shows, simultaneously created and erased the newly drawn national boundaries by building diasporas and 'de-territorialized' fractured identities across South Asia on the one hand, and by raising serious questions about the authenticity and citizenship of Partition migrants on the other. Through showing how the Sylhet Referendum and Partition live on in memory, this research highlights the importance of these two events in the spilling-over of the Sylheti from a local into a contested South Asian identity.

Perhaps for the first time in Partition historiography, memories of the 1947 Sylhet Referendum and Partition are retold in this book using oral narratives of both Sylheti Hindus and Muslims who migrated to Assam/India in the period 1947-50. The people interviewed for this research were themselves eyewitnesses of the Referendum and Partition. I have used the voices of Sylheti Hindus who had voted in favour of Sylhet's retention within India but following the referendum results had to migrate out of Sylhet in 1947-50; as well as Sylheti Muslims, most of whom had voted in favour of Sylhet joining East Pakistan but afterwards became, reluctantly or otherwise, citizens of the newly-formed Indian state. The oral testimony of these two groups of Sylhetis, who are now citizens of India, are used to reconstruct and analyse the Sylhet Referendum, Partition and its impact on the lives of ordinary peoples, and how they remember it 60-odd years later.

Given that most eyewitnesses of the 1947 Sylhet Referendum and Partition are about 80 years old now (many of them have already passed away), this research assumes greater importance as it documents hitherto unavailable primary data collected through interviews of these eyewitnesses which might otherwise have been completely lost by now. Their stories are, of course, set against the background of the wider issues of nationalism, communalism and Assam's own politics of culture that created conditions for the Partition of Sylhet long before 1947.

What makes Sylhet's case particularly interesting in Partition historiography is its unique history of being separated from East Bengal and attached to Assam for 70 years (1874-1947) by the colonial masters despite protests from Assamese and Sylhetis alike. It is this move that created the powerful local context for its eventual Partition. The idea of the Referendum may have been the result of the national context, or of Assam's inclusion in Jinnah's six-province vision of Pakistan. However, it is the local context that tells much of the real story—and explains the lack of a major outcry against Partition in northeast India, as it culled away most parts of a district that was unwelcome in Assam in the first place. However, even six decades later, the story of Sylhet remains caught within the acutely personal and 'closed' realms of Sylheti memory, nostalgia, imagination and living-room conversations. It is only since the turn of the new millennium that occasional attention through research papers started bringing the story of partition of Assam, and its unique experience, into the public realm. This book hopes to fill a bit of this gap in the overall Partition historiography.

CHAPTER ONE

Remembering Sylhet

PARTITION MIGRANTS: THE SYLHETIS AT ASSAM'S DOORS

My grandfather was one of the first natives of Sylhet district to arrive at the border of Assam after the Bengali-speaking Sylhet, which had been a part of Assam from 1874 until 1947, was ceded to East Pakistan on 15 August 1947, following a hurriedly organized and controversial[1] Referendum on 6-7 July that year. Little over a month earlier, on 3 June, Lord Louis Mountbatten, the last viceroy of India, had proposed that the plebiscite be held in order that the people of Sylhet (which was a Muslim-majority district in Hindu-majority Assam) could decide whether to stay in India or join Pakistan after Independence. The rest of Assam, it had been decided, would become a part of the newly Independent India. Following the decision to hold the Referendum, the Assam government offered its employees then posted in Sylhet the option to choose where they wanted to serve post-Partition—in India or Pakistan, regardless of the final outcome of the vote. In a letter dated 1 July 1947, the Chief Secretary to the Government of Assam informed all government employees, Indian as well as European, that they would be given 'an opportunity to select the government he wishes to serve', and asked them to furnish their option within one week in their own handwriting. The representatives of the two future governments, the Chief Secretary wrote, guaranteed existing terms and conditions of service, including retaining their job seniority.[2]

At the time of the Referendum, my grandfather was the sub-divisional police officer of Habiganj in Sylhet.[3] When the result was announced on the radio on 14 July in favour of Sylhet's inclusion in East Pakistan he informed the provincial government that he wanted to be relocated to Assam, in India. Word came in the late afternoon of 14 August, the day that the Assam government officially pulled out of Sylhet, that he was to immediately handover charge to his newly-appointed successor and move to a new posting in the hill township of Shillong, then the administrative capital of Assam. He quickly completed the formalities, and thereafter drove his wife and children from Habiganj to his ancestral home in Sylhet town, where his former colleagues urged him to stay back for just another day in order to watch the Independence Day celebrations. Thereafter, on the morning of 16 August 1947, the whole family made the five-hour drive up to Shillong, where my grandfather had purchased a house, Sanat Kutir, just five years earlier. Many years later while researching on Sylhet Partition migrants, I would be told that he was one of the 'luckier'[4] Assam government employees, who had been successfully relocated after the Referendum. Many other Sylhetis (as the natives of Sylhet are commonly known) on the other hand, who had made similar decisions found themselves without jobs upon arriving in Assam. There were 'no vacancies', they were told, and some were forced to undertake lengthy legal battles in order to be reinstated and retain their seniority.[5]

The 'optees' or the government employees who chose to relocate in India generally belonged to the English-educated middle class, or *bhadralok*—literally, 'gentlemen' or 'polite people'. This group originated in neighbouring Bengal (of which the

Bengali-speaking Sylhet was a part until 1874) during the colonial period, and was often employed in the colonial administration or in professions such as law, medicine, teaching, trade and the running of small businesses in colonial Assam after its annexation into the Raj in 1826. As interpreters, brokers to the English traders and go-betweens in judicial and revenue administration, they mediated between the British and the 'natives' in economic and administrative matters.[6] They had a liberal and secular outlook, a singular attachment to education, and a preference for white-collar jobs.[7] A majority of Partition optees from Sylhet were Hindu Bengali natives, with a smattering of Assamese Hindus from Assam proper or the Brahmaputra Valley (who were stationed in Sylhet at the time of the Referendum), which was the traditional homeland of the Assamese. According to one estimate,[8] about 1,800 Assam government employees based in Sylhet opted for service in Assam; according to another, the number was 1,492.[9] This group of government employees was among the first to follow the Assam government's official transfer out of Sylhet, partly because they wanted to, and partly because the provincial government had stated that it would not be responsible for those employees who had not received their transfer orders by 14 August 1947.

The optees, of course, constituted a very small fraction of Sylhet's Partition-displaced people. Many more Sylhetis of various backgrounds migrated to Assam between the years 1947 and 1950 just before major communal riots broke out in various parts of East Bengal, though not in Sylhet itself. According to a July 1949 census, there were already 24,600 families of displaced persons in Assam, or approximately 114,500 individuals,[10] a majority of whom were from Sylhet. The 1951 *Census of India* described this displaced population as belonging to the middle classes, intellectuals who were following the proceedings of the Constituent Assembly of Pakistan, or richer classes who could afford to come away.[11] In fact, the migration of Sylhetis to Assam in the 1947-50 period was considerably less when compared to the large-scale refugee inflow that followed the 1950 communal disturbances in Soneswar, Habiganj, North Mymensingh and Rajshahi, and the massive riots in East Bengal, particularly Dacca (now Dhaka). Rumours and fearful exaggerations of riots in other parts of Bengal created serious apprehension among people, prompting many to decide to leave Sylhet 'before anything worse happened'.

THE STORY OF SYLHET

Over the years, the story of my grandfather's move from Sylhet to Assam had become a part of our family folklore. Indeed, as far back as I can remember, stories about Sylhet had echoed around us, especially during trips to our old family home in Dibrugarh in northern Assam, where my grandmother spent most of her days after my grandfather died. This was not a conscious act, nor did anyone perhaps have the notion of being oral historians of the community. The stories were simply related in off-the-cuff manner—some by way of complaining about the present, while others were just idle gossip. My grand-mother's sentences often started with something along the lines of, 'If only your grandfather were still alive . . .' before moving on to a story about the prosperity and respect he had enjoyed during his time as a police officer in Sylhet and, later, Shillong and many other parts of Assam.

One of my grandmother's favourite stories took place at the time of the Referendum. At that time,

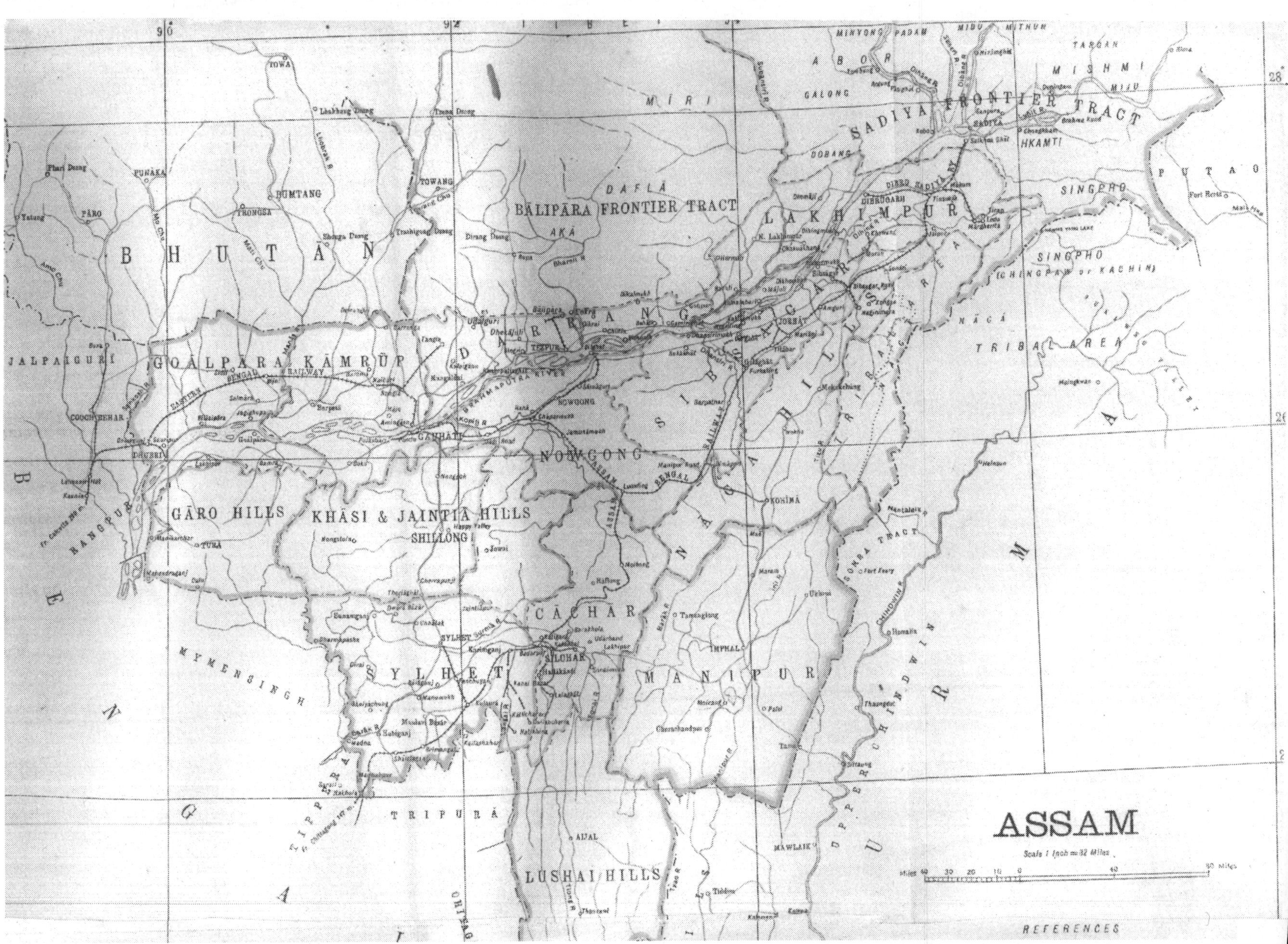

ASSAM
Scale 1 Inch = 32 Miles
REFERENCES
BHUTĀN
GOĀLPĀRA
KĀMRŪP
DARRANG
BĀLIPĀRA FRONTIER TRACT
SADIYA FRONTIER TRACT
LAKHIMPUR
SIBSAGAR
NOWGONG
GĀRO HILLS
KHĀSI & JAINTIĀ HILLS
SHILLONG
CĀCHAR
SYLHET
MANIPUR
LUSHAI HILLS
NĀGA HILLS
NĀGA TRIBAL AREA
MIRI
DAFLĀ
AKĀ
ABOR
MISHMI
SINGPHO
PUTAO
JALPAIGURI
COOCH BEHAR
MYMENSINGH
TRIPURĀ
BENGAL
BRAHMAPUTRA RIVER
ASSAM BENGAL RAILWAY
GAUHATI
TEZPUR
DIBRUGARH
SADIYA
IMPHAL
SILCHAR
KOHIMA
DHUBRI
TURA
AIJAL

my grandfather was not supplied with any additional police force, arms and ammunition, or armed personnel to assist him in responding to law-and-order disturbances in Habiganj. Even on the two days of the Referendum, he had only the usual 10 to 12 Assam Rifles personnel under his command. Even though his official quarters was threatened to be attacked by groups of angry young men roaming the streets, my grandmother would tell us, 'Your grandfather had only one personal double-barrelled gun during the entire time of the Referendum'—it made all of us shiver, trying to imagine the situation. The family elders recalled many other such stories, often with the intent of impressing something or another on us wide-eyed children. 'Such fish you would have never seen as we had in Sylhet,' they would tell us. 'Our gardens were as big as your football fields.'

Many of our relatives and friends also had their own interesting tales of how they had moved from Sylhet to Assam in the aftermath of Partition. But even as Sylhetis, now relocated in different parts of India (and the world) continue to hand down the stories of their painful and unexpected displacement to the younger generations, few professional historians have seriously engaged with the Sylheti experience of the 1947 Partition. Most well-known studies of Partition are either macro-histories, focusing on the vast political wrangle between the Indian National Congress and the Muslim League for political power; or are explorations of the two best-known Partition cases, those of Punjab and Bengal. Thus, even six decades later, the story of the Sylheti displacement continues to remain caught within the acutely personal realms of memory, nostalgia and imagination.

WHY SYLHET?

I must have been about ten years old when I first walked through the tall gates of the crumbling mansion (I called it *Lal Baari*, the Red House, because of its red tiled roof) in a busy and thickly populated neighbourhood of Guwahati, the capital of Assam since 1972. At that time, I lived with my parents in a newly-constructed double-storeyed house not far away; but the sheer size of the collapsing mansion, its tottering wooden pillars and verandas teeming with people at all times of the day—men, women and children of various ages and sizes—was intimidating enough to keep me from going anywhere near it during the course of the evening walks I took with my Khasi-speaking nanny, whom I fondly called *kong* or older sister. Many years later, reading American history as an undergraduate, I realized that the mansion had looked startlingly like the crowded nineteenth-century tenements of New York City.

Lal Baari seemed to have been lovingly built by someone experiencing an economic upswing, a long time ago. As time passed, perhaps it was the sheer unwieldiness of the massive building that led to its decay—or, as some people whispered, perhaps it was the result of warring descendants that kept it from either being sold or repaired due to possible legal complications. Either way, it seemed just to have been left to crumble. The structure had a colonial look, the roof similar to the drooping eaves of the colonial part of Assam's famed Cotton College, built in 1901; the ceiling too looked just as high, at least from the outside. The wooden pillars that held up the roof were brittle and timeworn, peeling off in places where the women often leant against in the evenings.

It therefore came as quite a surprise when, one evening, my father announced that we were going to take a walk to Lal Baari to meet his cousin, whom he called Subir *da* (the latter the Bengali honorific for 'older brother'). Neither my older brother nor I had ever been aware that any of our relatives actually lived there. I do not remember much of our walk to Lal Baari, but two distinct memories have stayed with me ever since. The first was the startling sight of so many people sharing the many tiny rooms of the building: the dark, dusty corridors were literally swarming with men, women and children. I remember being so unnerved by this that I hung on to my father's hands for the entire time it took us to walk through the main entrance and into the two small rooms in which Subir *Jethu* (father's elder brother) and his family of five lived.

My second memory is that of a large framed black-and-white photograph of Subir Jethu, taken a long time ago somewhere in Sylhet, where he had been born and where he had lived until Partition. It showed a handsome, energetic young man sitting astride a large black horse, dressed in the finery of the well-to-do and with a half-smile on his face as he swung his riding whip high in the air. I could not make the connection between the figure in the photograph and the thin, sad man before me, some quarter century later. On our way back home, I asked my father about the portrait. 'He was the son of a rich landowner in Sylhet,' my father told me. 'But when the 1950 Partition-era riots happened between the Hindus and Muslims, he had to flee for his life, leaving behind all his ancestral property. His family lost everything.' But why did he live in an old and cluttered place like Lal Baari, and not in a nicer house? My grandfather too had come from Sylhet after Partition, I argued with my father, so how is that we have a better house? 'Because as the only son of a rich *zamindar* in Sylhet, he did not bother to get himself a proper education,' replied my father. 'Those Sylhetis who were educated were able to build better lives for themselves after Partition, even though they lost land and other properties.'

That photograph of Subir Jethu was my earliest encounter with the ugly face of India's 1947 Partition. At the tender age of ten, I had little comprehension about Partition; nor did I have any idea of where Sylhet was located on the map of India. What I hazily understood, however, were some introductory lessons about Partition, and how differently it had impacted on my grandfather's life on the one hand and Subir Jethu's on the other. Later,

I came to know that a large number of other residents of Lal Baari had also 'come from Sylhet' after Partition. Slowly, through numerous dinner-table conversations with my father, I gradually began to understand how and why Partition affected so many people, and differently, depending on their family background, education, social networking and the timing of their move to India. Examples were easy to come by because we were Sylhetis ourselves, and many of our relatives and family friends had also 'come from Sylhet'. But few had fallen into such difficult times as Subir Jethu. In fact, most were quite well established: several of my father's childhood friends were professionals like him or held prestigious government jobs, while many others ran small businesses and could afford to send their children to the slightly more expensive English-medium schools that already abounded in Guwahati city during the early 1980s.

In this way, I became interested in the story of Sylhet long before I became a serious student of Indian history and eventually, a social history researcher. But the stories I had heard during my childhood were nearly always incomplete. The accounts were deeply personal and anecdotal, and no one really discussed the bigger picture as historians might have done. Surprisingly again, the history books I studied in school—history of India generally, as well as specifically of Assam—did not carry details of the 1947 Sylhet Partition either. My grandmother died when I turned twelve, and thereafter rest of my knowledge on the topic was primarily drawn from my father's stories, and stray conversations with extended family members. As the years passed, Sylhet became a mysterious place in my imagination from where people like us 'had come', but the details more or less stopped there. Over the following years, several questions kept dogging my mind. What does Sylhet look like? Where, indeed, is Sylhet? When was it partitioned, and why? Why were so many people like my grandfather and Subir Jethu forced to leave their ancestral homeland after Partition? As the years passed by, I went to the university and began to learn more about Indian history. Soon enough I found out that Partition, the break-up of colonial India in 1947, had been the subject of substantial historical research in recent times; but also that this work had almost exclusively focused on the experiences of the two border provinces of the Punjab and Bengal, which were partitioned after the two new sovereign states of India and Pakistan came into being. Remarkably little is known about yet other parts of India that were equally affected by Partition—tucked away in the far-eastern corner of India, one of them was the district of Sylhet. This was the reason why I had not found satisfactory answers to my questions in the school history books—so few people actually knew about it apart from the Sylhetis themselves!

I quickly learnt that Sylhet was a Bengali-speaking district in the Assamese-speaking province of Assam that balanced uneasily between its Hindu (38 per cent) and Muslim (60 per cent) populations on the eve of Partition. Following the Referendum of 6-7 July 1947 most of this district (barring a small Hindu pocket), became part of East Pakistan. Almost immediately afterwards, groups of Sylheti Hindus (including optees) left their homes and moved to the Indian-side of the border. According to eyewitnesses, some Sylheti Hindus fearing the worst had, in fact, left soon after the announcement of the Referendum was made on the radio and newspapers. After the widely publicized East Bengal communal clashes of 1950, a large number of Sylhetis (mostly Hindus) crossed the newly-created national borders into India helter-skelter in search of a safe living space. Conversely though, there were considerably smaller flows of Sylheti Muslims crossing over to East Pakistan from Assam at that time.

The research that I tried to put together in this book is based on the memories of the Sylhet Referendum and Partition of those groups of Sylhetis (both Hindus and Muslims) who migrated to India in the period 1947-50—that is, before the large-scale migration took place in 1950; all the people interviewed for this research were themselves eyewitnesses of the Referendum and Partition. I used the voices of the Sylheti Hindus (*bhadralok*) who had voted in favour of Sylhet's retention within India but who later had to leave Sylhet after the Referendum result was announced; as well as Sylheti Muslims of the Karimganj area (the Hindu pocket that was retained in India in 1947), many of whom had voted in favour of Sylhet joining East Pakistan but were forced to stay back in the newly-formed India due to circumstances discussed later in the book. The oral testimony of these two groups of Sylhetis are used to reconstruct and analyse the Sylhet Referendum, Partition and its impact on the lives of the ordinary people, and how the two communities remember and recount it 60-odd years afterwards. These stories, of course, are set against the background of the wider issues of nationalism, communalism and Assam's own identity politics that created conditions for the Partition of Sylhet long before 1947.

PARTITION IN PUNJAB AND BENGAL

In her first novel, *The Pakistani Bride*, celebrated Pakistani writer Bapsi Sidhwa gives a blow-by-blow account of the violence that took place on the streets of north India immediately following Partition. Some of this was carried out mindlessly by an enraged mob, such as the powerful scenes in which Muslim passengers were drawn from a Lahore-bound train and mercilessly butchered. 'Now the mob runs towards the train with lighted torches,' Sidhwa writes, 'A Sikh, hair streaming, lashed a bloody wound. Another slowly waved a child stuck at the end of his spear like a banner.'[12] She goes on to describe the violence that ultimately makes one of her characters, Sikandar, crumple to the ground, 'astonished by the blood gushing from his stomach' as a woman tramples over him, more and more legs trampling him until he 'mercifully feels no pain'. Yet another character, an ethnic Kohistani named Qasim, took advantage of this atmosphere of tension and fear to settle an old rivalry with his Hindu employer. Later, sitting atop a Lahore-bound train, Qasim boasted to another passenger that just before getting on the train he had killed a *babu*, a government clerk, simply because he was a Hindu.

It was not accounts such as these, however, but rather the large-scale, national macro-histories that largely shaped the popular understanding of Partition long before the 1980s, when historians decided to change tracks and take up the task of telling the 'real' and 'human' stories of 1947. Instead, in the aftermath of Partition it were the novelists, short-story writers, filmmakers and poets who were writing down these accounts. Most academic engagements with Partition remained mired in high politics and personalities, much in the tradition of nationalistic historiography, at a time when volumes after volumes were produced on the lives of Mahatma Gandhi, Jawaharlal Nehru and Vallabhbhai Patel, their leadership and contribution to India's Independence. In these nationalistic depictions of India's 'tryst with destiny', there was little philosophical or methodological space to accommodate the details of how the lives of ordinary people were impacted by this momentous event; nor were the deeply personal stories of Partition considered historical enough for professional historians.

This predominantly elitist and nationalistic style of historiography worldwide began to shift focus with the advent of social historians, with their variegated ideas regarding the purpose and methodology of writing history. Historians from diverse fields threw up new ideas: the Annalistes, for instance, who claimed that history should be studied along with other social sciences in order to be 'total'; or the Marxists, who championed a 'history from below'; or the postmodernists, who declared that social practices determined the writing of history which itself was a powerful site for contestation of meanings. Some groups began to attempt newer ways of writing colonial history in general, and Indian history in particular, in which they used the Western historiography prototype to confront the colonial renderings of vernacular histories. A leading figure in this 'movement' was then-Australia-based Bengali historian Ranajit Guha, who provided some of the seminal criticism of colonial historiography of India. The publication of his pathbreaking work *Elemen-*

tary Aspects of Peasant Insurgency in India (1983) opened a floodgate of new historical works by many other historians, especially those with whom he created a powerful new school of historiography, the Subaltern group.

Since 1982, this formidable group of South Asianists has produced 12 volumes of 'new history', which have challenged both the philosophy and methodology of 'elitist' histories of colonial India. The works of Gyanendra Pandey, one of the leading subaltern historians, has provided a powerful critique of India's Partition historiography and focused on rewriting some of it. Such interpretations, originally inspired by the works of Marxist scholar Antonio Gramsci and later based mostly on postmodernism, have found a growing popularity over the years, along with a fair measure of criticism albeit, among younger historians. It has also been aided by the works of several other eminent historians who are not a part of the subaltern studies project but share similar views regarding the use of newer sources to study Partition. Perhaps, inspired by the Holocaust historians, these individuals have creatively re-read some existing sources and used unconventional or popular sources and methodologies to write a different kind of Partition history than was previously available. In this, interviews based on memories of eyewitnesses, gradually emerged as a new and precious tool. Following the publication of these new histories,[13] there gradually emerged a systematic critique of Partition historiography from a variety of angles: that previous works were 'elitist', that they presented Partition as a 'macro-political event' or 'personal disaster', even a 'male' experience, or that they focused solely on the 'communities of suffering'.

Many historians now began to use non-traditional sources such as memories, folk histories and popular fiction to write about the 'unheard'. They worked to turn what Ranajit Guha called the 'small voices' into pages of history, and to shed new light on the everyday lives of common peoples thrown into turmoil before, during and after Partition. These works helped to flesh out the heterogeneity and unevenness in Partition experiences, thus generating a debate—from the short stories of Lahore's Saadat Hasan Manto's to the reminiscences of East Bengal by Calcutta's Sunil Gangopadhyay. A spate of popular Bollywood films such as *Earth*, *Mammo*, *Ghadar* and others likewise attempted to understand how

Partition unfolded in its local context and impacted the lives of ordinary people.

This change could quickly be seen within the mainstream as well. In 1997, on the 50th anniversary of Partition, some of India's leading English-language news magazines published thematic issues on Partition that included hard-hitting human-interest stories dealing with issues such as separated families, violence, loss and pain. Some web-based discussion groups also made special efforts to compile and circulate stories of Hindu-Muslim friendships, both before and after 1947.[14] Sunil Gangopadhyay has periodically been writing evocative articles and stories about Partition, while Ritwik Ghatak's popular films or Bhupen Hazarika's legendary rendering of *Ganga aamar ma . . . Padma aamar ma* (The Ganges is my mother, so is the Padma) often brought back memories of the pre-Partition friendships, connections and continuities. Besides an avalanche of Indian television serials based on the theme of Partition during the 1980s and 1990s, excellent compilations of short stories too have recently brought the human impact of Partition firmly within the popular realm. Scholars such as Kathinka Sinha-Kerkoff, Ishtiaq

Ahmed, Joya Chatterji and Ravinder Kaur,[15] to name just a few, and the popular Bollywood film *Veer-Zaara*, have gone to great lengths to show how Partition continues to impact lives around South Asia even after half-century and more.

Hemanga Biswas (1912–87), one of Sylhet's best-known poets, freedom fighter and leftist intellectual, expressed the sorrow and pain of Partition in his soulful poetry. Biswas had a great talent for incorporating patriotism into the many genres of folk songs of East Bengal, for instance *Aamar mon kande-re Padma-r chorer laigya* (My heart cries for the islands on the river Padma) or *Aamar obhagya-r ontor kande-re pora desher laigya* (My unlucky heart cries out for my poor country).[16] Sylhet did not have a Saadat Hasan Manto like Punjab did, but in the works of Hemanga Biswas, whose songs are still popular among Sylhetis, one can still locate the heartrending sadness of Partition in the simple, straightforward, everyday Sylheti language. Voices such as his, which focused on the intensely personal, were widely different from the historical accounts, which focused on the bigger picture instead. This disjuncture between the ordinary peoples and historians represents a significant gap in Partition studies, one that must be filled in quickly by including eyewitness accounts in the historian's repertoire of sources.

'[T]he historical narrative we were taught in school', writes novelist Amit Chaudhuri in his essay 'Partition as Exile', 'with its emphasis on Partition and freedom, did not accentuate or define, in my mind, my parents' experiences and lives, and my own place as a child of people displaced from their homeland; if anything, it suppressed such formulations.'[17] This is hardly surprising. Elsewhere I have pointed out that many eyewitnesses of the Sylhet Referendum and Partition did not consider their testimonies to be 'historical', and asked me instead to speak with historians or government officials 'who were there'.[18] This disjuncture was specifically underlined by another eyewitness during an interview in India in 2007, who asked, *Partitioner kotha ekhon aabar boi-er theke portay hobe naki? Aami nijer chokhe Partition dekhechhi* (Do I have to read about Partition from books now? I have seen Partition with my own eyes). Over the following two years of my research, many others echoed such sentiments. Thus, at times the very linear and objective trajectory of historical studies seemed to alter the meaning of Partition for the eyewitnesses who had experienced Partition in person—and, often, remembered it quite differently, in fragments, perhaps, and on a small scale that rarely extended beyond a village, city, family or circle of friends. For them, Partition did not exist in meta-narratives, but rather in micro-narratives located within individual life spans, which often had little in common with the public nature of the written histories.

WRITING ABOUT PARTITION

In her recently published book *Since 1947: Partition Narratives among Punjabi Migrants of Delhi*, Ravinder Kaur suggests that the process of migration and resettlement was experienced by different sections of society at multiple levels, and that no single narrative can therefore claim to represent the Partition 'reality'.[19] The multiplicity of the Partition experience, and the growing need for field-based studies of Partition, is likewise highlighted by Mushirul Hasan, Urvashi Butalia, Jasodhara Bagchi and Shubhoranjan Dasgupta, among other well-known historians and social scientists. Historians Mahbubur Rahman and Willem Van Schendel also argue in their essay 'I Am Not a Refugee: Rethinking Partition Migration'[20] that our understanding of Partition is 'still boxed in by a number of set approaches',[21] one of which is the focus on 'Partition-in-the-west',[22] referring to what took place in western India (or the Punjab), which has come to figure as 'a model of sorts, a shorthand for what Partition entailed, the prime case from which to draw general conclusions'.[23] In this way, they note, 'some particular images of refugees have come to be associated with Partition'[24] that are primarily drawn from case studies from the Punjab. Thus, Rahman and Van Schendel conclude that studies on the 1947 Partition have not yet taken into consideration the multiple experiences of Partition migrants, and therefore the construction of Partition migrants remains trapped within a set of given parameters.

In a 2001 essay published in *Contemporary South Asia*,[25] I discussed how the Sylheti *bhadralok* can be said to be exceptions to the general image of Partition migrants, one that came to be based primarily on the experience of Partition-in-the-west and, to a lesser extent, Bengal. In fact, by shifting the focus a bit, the 'local' contexts of the 1947 Partition—and there were many—offered crucial assistance to explaining the nuances of each of the different Partition sites. Of course, this is not to undermine the national and imperial contexts of Partition, but rather to simultaneously take into account the local political, economic and social realities in which much of the Partition experience was embedded. Indeed, this could well explain why the experiences of Partition in Bengal or Sylhet were different both from one another and from what took place in the Punjab, particularly when it came to levels of violence, conditions of out-migration and post-Partition settlement strategies.

It should be reiterated that the 1947 Partition generated uneven manifestations, diverse responses and varying levels of violence in different areas across which the new national borders were drawn. The variegated responses to Partition mostly depended on factors such as the extent of politicization, communalization and group economic disparities, and were powerfully influenced by the local context of the concerned site, in addition to the overall national and imperial contexts of Partition. Moreover, not everyone was affected equally, or to the same extent, by the events of Partition. Yet as noted earlier, the special focus on the Punjab and Bengal has boxed the understanding of the Partition experience into a set mould, one primarily defined by large-scale violence, flight for life and destitution. In other, more far-flung locations, though, Partition experiences have developed in interestingly different ways.

One unifying theme in the surge of new histories and other popular works has been a desire to resurrect the experience of Partition by a 're-living' of the violence that, in the well-known words of Gyanendra Pandey, 'surrounded, accompanied and constituted Partition'.[26] Scholars are today using oral histories, memories and imaginative readings of historical and popular texts to recapture the 'tremendous human cost, the dispossession and anguish of millions, and the violence and brutalities', and the haunting memories of 'the smell of burning flesh, and screams of the victims of the 1947 riots'.[27] But in spite of the vast, extremely rich writings and critiques, this approach has still fallen short of providing a wide-ranging view of the enormous population movements across India's newly created borders. In these writings, Partition migrants have primarily been constructed as 'refugees' living the 'horror of Partition, the anguish and sorrow, pain and brutality of the riots of 1946-7', or innocent victims of 'communal passions and riotous mobs'. While these are undeniably powerful works, the imagery thrown up by these and other 'new histories' have come to appropriate the meaning of Partition and its migrants in a way in which violence, flight and destitution play a defining role.

With time, some scholars began to turn their attention from Partition in the west to Partition in eastern India, but their work again was subsumed by the Bengal experience now. Few historians turned their attention further to the east to Northeast India, and the focus of most of these historical works was 'strongly on metropolitan Calcutta and on refugee camps'.[28] Shubhoranjan Dasgupta and Jasodhara Bagchi point out that the nature of the Bengal Partition was different from the Partition of Punjab in some very crucial ways. Their edited volume *The Trauma and the Triumph: Gender and Partition in Eastern India* (2003) on the impact of Partition in India's eastern region, or Bengal, indeed manages to liberate the eastern Indian experience from much of what Van Schendel and Rahman call 'Punjabo-centrism'.[29] Upon a closer examination, however, the representation of the Bengali Partition migrant in 1947, with some notable exceptions, likewise remained trapped within the framework of violence, flight and destitution—the 'riot refugee',[30] a crucial though not the only type of Partition migration that took place after 1947.

Still, in spite of this similarity with the Punjab case studies, the above-mentioned work, taken together with some other scattered resources on Partition in the east, do manage to convince readers that the Bengal experience of Partition had its own unique nuances. However, many Partition scholars in the east continue to see an 'amazing silence'[31] on the Bengal Partition, and it is indeed true that more research has to be carried out on the topic before we are able to reach a definitive understanding of the meanings of the Bengal Partition. Rahman and Van Schendel, for instance, have stressed the need for additional research 'before we can say anything in general about Partition refugees in eastern South Asia', and point out that such work is likely to focus on individuals beyond the compass of conventional refugee studies in the region.[32] They also caution against an indiscriminate use of the term *refugee* for all those who crossed borders post-Partition. In their categorization of five different types of border-crossers in 1947, only one is characterized as 'refugees from interior' or 'riot refugees', who most closely resemble the archetypal refugee offered by most of the literature on the issue.[33]

Against this background it might be rewarding to look into another site, in the British Indian province of Assam, where Partition unfolded at the same time as in the Punjab and Bengal. What might an enquiry into the 1947 Sylhet Referendum and Partition add to the above understanding of Partition? Was the experience largely similar with regards to patterns of violence and displacement, or did events unfold somewhat differently and in relative isolation in this far off corner of British India? Assam was a province that rarely made news in British India other than for its tea production, but it eventually became included in Mohammed Ali Jinnah's demand for a six-province Pakistan. While the point of entry into the Partition experience necessarily has to be the violence and tragedy associated with involuntary dislocation, as in the Punjab and Bengal cases, it is equally important to know the histories of other such communities who may have experienced Partition at almost the same time as in these other two places—but in far different ways.

This book is an attempt to integrate Sylhet's forgotten story into the growing new and more 'mainstream' histories of India's Partition. Besides filling an obvious gap in Partition historiography, it hopes to carry forward the genre of the new history by telling the story through the Sylheti voice. Besides using voices collected from interviews conducted with eyewitnesses of the Sylhet Referendum and Partition, in places I have drawn from autobiographies, memoirs and even internet sources that likewise capture the Sylheti voice across 2 or 3 generations. This research allows for the presence of both Sylheti Hindu and Muslim voices, without which Partition appears to be about a tragedy of just one community alone. More importantly, there might be a difference in the way that Hindu and Muslim Sylhetis choose to remember the events of 1947.

Again, if we accept that the Sylhet Partition was not as violent as the Partition-era events were elsewhere, we might be tempted to ask, rather speculatively, whether there has been enough delving into those Punjab and Bengal Partition migrants who, too, did not experience direct violence. Hence, this research might even be used to extrapolate and make a point for Bengal and the Punjab as well, as an aside, even if such an endeavour is not central to this work. A clarification also has to be made at the outset that as a researcher I am of Sylheti-Hindu origin myself and that besides being an academic exercise, this is also a personal journey into my own roots. As a third-generation member of the Indian Hindu Sylheti community, it has not always been easy for me to separate my complex and multi-layered lived experience among other Sylhetis in Assam from the more scientific and academic rigueur of fieldwork. This has often led me to alternate between the role of subject and researcher, and to interweave a narrative that sometimes oscillates between the two. As a 'new historian'[34] who is comfortable with her own positionality within a discourse, I can only hope that this will help to enrich the present study.

NOTES

1. See Amalendu Guha, *Planter Raj to Swaraj: Freedom Struggle and Electoral Politics in Assam, 1826-1947*, New Delhi: Indian Council of Historical Research, 1977, pp. 261-2; Sujit Chaudhuri, 'A God-sent Opportunity', www.india-seminar.com/2002/510/510%20sujit%20 chaudhuri.htm, 2002, retrieved on 5 November 2007; Bidyut Chakrabarty, 'The "Hut" and "Axe": The 1947 Sylhet Referendum', *Indian Economic and Social History Review*, 39(4), pp. 317-50; Makhan Lal Kar, *Muslims in*

Assam's Politics, New Delhi: Vikas, 1997, pp. 48-9.

2. K.B. Mukherjee, 'A Great Betrayal', in Nihar Ranjan Datta and Mihir Kanti Datta (eds), *Adhyapak Digindra Chandra Datta-r Janma Satabarshiki Swarani*, Calcutta: no publisher, 2000, p. 48.
3. I had mistakenly written that he was the last Superintendent of Police of Sylhet in A. Dasgupta, 'Denial and Resistance: Sylheti Partition "Refugees" in Assam', *Contemporary South Asia*, 10(3), 2001, pp. 343-60. He was indeed posted in Sylhet town in 1946, but after a few months he was transferred to Habiganj where he worked until 14 August 1947 before opting to migrate to Assam.
4. Interviews and e-mail discussions with Sylheti Hindu Partition migrants in India and the United States. One of them communicated in course of several e-mail discussions that the reason why my grandfather had been 'so lucky' to be successfully relocated was that 'the Assam police force was short of police officers and feared [attacks from] the Khasis'. That is why, he said, the Sylheti police officers who opted for India did not generally face problems in being reinstated in Assam/India after 1947, unlike those in other services, particularly, higher education.
5. According to the same interviewee (above) his father had to fight a five-year court battle to be reinstated in his job in the higher-education sector. He also gave examples of several other government college teachers from Sylhet who had opted to serve in India, but found themselves without jobs upon arrival as there were 'no vacancies'. Many such stories were also collected during the interviews.
6. Frederick C. Thomas, *Calcutta Poor: Elegies on a City Above Pretense*, New York: M.E. Sharpe, 1997, p. 25.

7. Ibid.
8. J.K. Choudhury, *Memorandum Submitted to States' Reorganization Commission by Cachar States Reorganization Committee*, Silchar: Cachar States Reorganization Committee, 1954.
9. Mukherjee, 2000, op. cit., p. 59.
10. *Census of India 1951*, Assam, Manipur and Tripura, Government of India, p. 356.
11. Ibid.
12. Bapsi Sidhwa, *The Pakistani Bride*, Minnesota: Milkweed Editions, 2008, p. 25.
13. Some interesting examples of research on Partition are Suvir Kaul, *The Partitions of Memory: The Afterlife of the Division of India*, New Delhi: Permanent Black, 1999; Ritu Menon and Kamla Bhasin, *Borders and Boundaries: Women in India's Partition*, New Delhi: Kali for Women, 1998; Gyanendra Pandey, *The Construction of Communalism in Colonial North India*, New Delhi: Oxford University Press, 1990; Gyanendra Pandey, *Remembering Partition: Violence, Nationalism and History in India*, Cambridge: Cambridge University Press, 1998; Dipesh Chakravarty, 'Remembered Villages: Representations of Hindu-Bengali memories in the aftermath of the Partition', *Economic and Political Weekly*, 10 August 1996.
14. Asiapeace is one such web-based group. There are many others available and in circulation.
15. Ravinder Kaur, *Since 1947: Partition Narratives among Punjabi Migrants of Delhi*, New Delhi: Oxford University Press, 2007.
16. Hena Das, 'Hemanga Biswas O' Srihatt-e Gananatya Andolan', in S. Debray (ed.), *Sribhumi Srihatta: Sreehat-*

ter Samskriti Bishayak Prabandha Samkalan, Durgapur: Durgapur Srihatta Sammilani, 1995. (Translation from Bengali mine.)

17. Amit Chaudhuri, 'Partition as Exile', http://www.telegraphindia.com/1000709/editoria.htm retrieved on 3 May 2008.
18. Anindita Dasgupta, 'Remembering Sylhet: A Forgotten Story of India's 1947 Partition, *The Economic and Political Weekly*, 43(31) 2008, pp. 18-22.
19. Kaur, *Since 1947: Partition Narratives among Punjabi Migrants of Delhi*, op. cit.
20. Mahbub-ul Rahman and Willem Van Schendel, 'I Am Not a "Refugee": Rethinking Partition Migration'. *Modern Asian Studies*, 37(3), 2003, pp. 551-84.
21. Ibid., p. 551.
22. Ibid., p. 552.
23. Ibid.
24. Ibid., p. 554.
25. Anindita Dasgupta, 'Denial and Resistance: Sylheti Partition "Refugees" in Assam', *Contemporary South Asia*, 10(3), 2001, pp. 343-60.
26. Gyanendra Pandey, 'The Prose of Otherness', in D. Arnold and D. Hardiman (eds), *Subaltern Studies: Writings on South Asian History and Society*, vol. 8, London: Oxford University Press, pp. 188-221.
27. Ishtiaq Ahmed, 'The Lahore Effect', *Seminar*, http://www.india-seminar.com/2006/567/567_ishtiaq_ahmed.htm retrieved on 7 January 2008.
28. Rahman and Van Schendel, 2003, op. cit., p. 555.
29. Ibid., p. 580.
30. Ibid., p. 566.

31. See Santanu Sanyal's review of *Bengal Partition Stories: An Unclosed Chapter*, ed. Bashabi Fraser, available at ttp://www.thehindubusinessline.com/life/2007/02/02/stories/2007020200140400.htm retrieved on 16/5/2007
32. Rahman and Van Schendel, 2003, op. cit., p. 556.
33. Ibid., pp. 557-60.
34. The term 'new history' from the French term *nouvelle histoire*, was coined by historians Jacques Le Goff and Pierre Nora of the Annales School in France in the 1970s. The movement rejected the traditional ways of writing history which focused on 'grand politics' and 'great men'. It was primarily concerned with individuals' motivations and intentions as explanatory factors for historical events and recognized the value of subjectivity of the historian.

CHAPTER TWO

History and Memory, for Hindus and Muslims

The relationship between memory and history has dominated debates within the discipline of history since the work of the Annales School of historians in France from the early twentieth century. What, indeed, is the difference between history and memory? Generally speaking, the two terms are related but do have different meanings. History (*Histoire* in French, with an upper-case *h*) relates to a more or less objective sequence of events, often about or related to living entities: the history of my father, my city, my country, of religion, of the universe, of art, etc. The French *une histoire*, with a lower case, is also used, but only in reference to 'a story', which is of course quite different. Memory (*mémoire* in French), on the other hand, is more subjective, as it generally relates to the representation that we, individually or collectively, can have about those events. As such, we can consider that memory timespan is shorter than history, and that we can lose our memories about actual history. We can also speak of '*mémoire* collective' that is owned and transmitted by the members of a community from generation to generation. Ultimately, both words can be used for the same concept in literature or spoken language—for instance, the French phrase *ecrire ses mémoires* literally means 'writing about its own history'; in effect, though, it means that we write about what we remember—or want to remember.

In the discipline of history, however, a storytelling 'subject' is central to memories, meaning that a narrative has a narrator who makes a decision about what to remember. This subjectivity itself makes such narratives generally questionable to professional historians, as the debate swings between the pure subjectivity of memories and the near objectivity of history. That memory is subjective, eclectic and almost primarily a product of present politics is also a powerful argument brought against using memory as a primary source in historiography. Therefore, it might be argued that history and memory are in reality two entirely separate activities.

The French historian Pierre Nora begins by drawing a sharp distinction between the two. 'Memory is life, borne by societies founded in its name,' he states. 'It remains in permanent evolution, open to the dialectic of remembering and forgetting, unconscious of its successive deformations, vulnerable to manipulation and appropriation, susceptible to being long dormant, and periodically revived.'[1] History, on the other hand, 'is the reconstruction, always problematic and incomplete, of what is no longer'.[2] Following this relatively succinct distinction, however, Nora goes on to state that the environment in which 'real memory' operates has been dislodged 'under the pressure of a fundamental historical sensibility. Thus, what is remembered assumes orderliness and specificity that bring memory under the province of history.'[3] George Lipsitz and Toni Morrison have worked with the idea of a 'counter-memory' of African-Americans, which Lipsitz defines as 'looking into the past for hidden histories of those excluded from dominant narratives'.[4]

Among the current generation of historians, there is a growing belief that in some sense the available history is not genuine or democratic, and that these firsthand eyewitnesses will add an element of authenticity to historical accounts. In such case, memories could also be a counterpart to history and tell a parallel story—one that runs alongside the historians' history, closing the cracks and gaps, much like the 'putty of memory' between the 'bricks of history'. Still, it is never easy to work with memories. Some people remember more readily than others, while others feel that their personal memories are too insignificant and thus not worth remembering. Some simply do not remember; some others do not want to walk down memory lane, preferring to forget. So does this kind of memory have the ability to produce a narrative that is authentic, dependable and verifiable? If not, is it still worth 'writing memory' as opposed to 'writing history'?

Through memories, however, one can strive for stories that are truly personal, and that go much deeper emotionally than the more impersonal and objective works of history. These stories are not what one might expect to read in a history book, but ones that can be told only to trusted friends over the course of intimate conversations. These stories present complex and fuller accounts, and provide the readers an opportunity to meet, almost personally as it were with real people to whom real things happened. In her book *The Other Side of Silence*, Urvashi

Butalia writes: 'I have come to believe that there is no way we can begin to understand what Partition was about, unless we look at how people remember it.'[5] Therefore, the choice of this methodology in the current book has been not to create a 'counter-narrative', but, in the words of G.M. Trevelyn, 'I do this knowing that others are still engaged in the writing of conventional political history'.[6] As such, what this research tries to do is, to borrow the words of Urvashi Butalia, is 'to offer a way of turning the historical lens at a somewhat different angle, and to look at what this perspective offers'.[7] And so, in this work, memory becomes the handmaiden of history.

Like many other displaced communities around the world, the 'Sylheti' in India is almost entirely an oral identity; storytelling is crucial to this identity being transmitted across generations. Like other diasporas or 'scattered people', Sylheti elders have always told stories about their life and times in pre-Partition Sylhet to the younger generation, and handed over their own customs, traditions, language, etc., to them. Two words in the title of this book express the centrality of oral transmission in the Sylheti identity: *remembering* denotes that this work is an act of remembrance by both the researcher and the respondents; *story* invokes a Sylheti narrative in which the Sylhetis themselves choose to remember or forget the memories of Sylhet. This research, therefore, can be seen as capturing the history of a memory, or as being the memory of a history. It also becomes ethnohistory or the history of a people, though a kind of history that has not yet been archived officially.

On the issue of validity, what is most important is that the narrators consider their stories to be true—as a researcher, I am interested in all the ways that the past is narrated, regardless of whether it is factual. There are reasons, after all, for what and how people remember; the interpretation of the tale is what is critical, not the tale itself. For this research, I not only believed that the Sylheti past could be seen through a number of different lenses, but that there also could be significant differences between the Hindu and Muslim communities in the ways in which the Referendum and Partition are remembered or forgotten. No less crucial is how ethnic and individual memories alter perceptions of the past and, by implication, the writing of history. Thus, what follows needs to be seen as an attempt to explore the politics of history.

SEARCHING FOR SYLHETIS

Finding eyewitnesses of the Sylhet Referendum and Partition for this research was both easy as well as difficult. The ease was due to the sheer numbers of my extended family members and friends with whom I could effortlessly spend hours discussing and bonding. Therefore, much of the interviews I carried out were done using what researchers would call 'snowball sampling', in which one interviewee would often direct me to the next one. Unfortunately, many of the eyewitnesses of the Sylhet Partition (around 80 years old at the time of interviews) had either passed away or had moved to different parts of the country or abroad. In fact, had I started my work about 10 or 15 years back I might still have been able to resurrect life stories of remarkable people who had themselves played active roles during the Sylhet Referendum and Partition or had known others who had. I now remember that when I was growing up in Assam, many such people had actually been known to my parents or grandparents, and deeply regret that at that time I was too young to ask them about the roles that they had played during the Referendum and Partition. So, I feel that whatever accounts I have been able to collect and publish in this book, while a mere drop in the ocean, yet represents the fast-disappearing memories of an entire generation of Sylhetis who had lived through momentous times like the Partition—an event which is far closer to my own imagination than the faraway Punjab, and even neighbouring Bengal, where my mother was born and raised. And it was people like the interviewees who connected me to the happenings of a distant past—my own past—because they 'had been there' themselves. Through their stories, the events like the July Referendum and Partition gradually began to create their own meanings into my life in intimate ways. In this research I thus make an attempt to document some of the voices that are still available before this generation passes away into the twilight, taking with them stories about the homeland they had long left behind.

But if I had expected many of the interviewees to be confused, or their memories of 1947 to be garbled, I was to be proved profoundly mistaken. Most of them insisted on giving me the exact dates of events, names of individuals involved, and places where specific incidents had occurred, even after I clarified that I was not looking for such precise information. In my father, who often accompanied me to these interviews, many of the interviewees found a friend, a younger Sylheti, and were comfortable enough to talk about the past.

Before moving into the results of these conversations, it will be interesting to compare my fieldwork experience with that of Meenakshie Verma, a young researcher who also used oral history to write an insightful history of Partition violence and how people have remembered it in the Punjab.[8] As a researcher of the same generation, researching a similar topic using similar methodology, I could not help but be struck by the vastly different experience that the two of us seemed to have had in the course of our respective fieldwork. Here I touch only on two differences that are important for my current work.

First, Verma notes that within the families that she interviewed most of the storytelling or transmissions about Partition occurred mainly in moments of 'delirium, but seldom as a conscious act of sharing the past or narrating an event'.[9] This could hardly be farther from the reality of the Sylhetis. My father was about ten years old at the time of the Referendum and Partition, when my grandfather left his then-official posting at Sylhet. As mentioned before, stories about Sylhet had always reverberated around us, especially in our ancestral home in Dibrugarh—told either by my grandmother, my five uncles, my father or the scores of other family members and friends. Further, in the course of my fieldwork, whenever I donned the mantle of the social historian I found the older generation of Sylhetis to be forthcoming, regardless of whether I knew them personally or did not. Some were just happy to reminisce; some became in many ways unwitting oral historians of their own community, and were eager that the nearly-forgotten story be retold and quickly written down. Others were simply happy that a representative of the younger generation was taking an interest in what they had to say.

Second, 'violence' has been a missing theme in the predominantly *bhadralok* Sylheti Hindu narratives. While there indeed was 'nostalgia', as Verma also notes in her book, there was comparatively less 'trauma' associated with their memories of 1947. In fact, most Sylheti Hindus did not use the word 'violence' in their storytelling with me. At best there were hazy references to some instances of violence being inflicted on 'others'; but as noted previously, besides cases of a few petty thefts or land encroachment by people of the other faith, none could provide me with any instance of communal violence that they had seen, experienced personally or even read about in the newspapers of the time. Verma describes, how the names of cities had become "metaphors for tear, anguish, suffering and violence" and how they "fleeted in and out of experiences and chimeras".[10] On the other hand, what stood out in the Sylheti Hindu narratives was no chimera but a spirit of resignation backed by a sense of having been deceived by opportunistic politicians—and, in the final analysis, of having been abandoned by all in 1947.

To identify and interview Sylheti Muslims was undoubtedly a more difficult task, but one made somewhat easier by my very able research assistant, Khaleda Sultana, of Sylheti Muslim origin herself. Khaleda too looked within her own community of relatives and friends in the Karimganj, Hailakandi and Patharkandi areas of the Barak Valley, in order to identify eyewitnesses and secure their consent to being interviewed. Many of the Sylheti Muslims, with whom we spoke, felt that the Muslims who remained in India after Partition were either 'mostly satisfied here or could not get due place in East Pakistan'. We were told that there were some Muslims who went to Pakistan[11] at the time of Partition but came back again, as they were unable to find sustainable livelihood options there. A large number of those who were able to find work had been farmers or held lower-end government jobs at the time of Partition. I quickly realized that this would become a problem for my analysis later, as the Sylheti Hindu eyewitnesses would end up being viewed as mostly middle class and professional, while the Sylheti Muslims would be viewed as mostly socio-economically 'backward'. But given that we were constrained by the fact that it was extremely difficult to identify Partition eyewitnesses, we generally could not be too choosy.

After a series of interviews, Khaleda felt that the interview responses would differ on the basis of a person's current life, economic condition and other such factors. Some Muslims who decided not to migrate to East Pakistan at the time of Partition told us that it would have been better had they left at that time instead, as new challenges (communal riots, violence) were 'waiting for the coming generation' who were now living in Assam. They also mentioned some recent cases of violence against Muslims in various districts of Assam, such as Dhubri and Sonitpur, as many were suspected of being undocumented migrants from neighbouring Bangladesh with whom the Bengali-speaking Muslims of Assam shared the same ethnicity and language. Pretty much like their Hindu counterparts, the Muslims were also not particularly emotional during the interviews, though they were less willing to speak to us, nor were they clearly aware of the historical importance of their narratives like the former. There were some angry outbursts as well during Khaleda's interview sessions, though once again 'violence' was not one of the principal elements in their story-telling. There was, on the other hand, a profound sense of regret about what had happened to the Sylheti Muslims in 1947, and occasional doubts were cast over if they had indeed taken the right decision in 'staying back' in India. What Khaleda and I felt was that the Sylheti Muslims were caught in an emotional dilemma—the regrets were more due to their current socio-economic or political situation rather than a sense of having made a historically wrong decision in 1947. Others wished that if at all Sylhet had to go to East Pakistan in 1947, it would have been better if the entire Bengali-speaking district had gone altogether. If not, then all of Sylhet should have stayed back in India.

Thus, decades after Partition, our interviewees, both Hindus and Muslims, expressed a mixed way of remembering the day of Partition. Though almost all of them stated that it was an event that should not have occurred, they were more interested in discussing on what grounds Partition had happened (though many were largely ignorant of the macro-level politics of 1947). Most of the cooperative interviewees pointed out that there were not many instances of communal clashes in Sylhet at the time. But after the Referendum, they said, the situation changed 'as it is a natural mindset to think that your people have tortured us, and so will do the same to you we once it is our turn'. Khaleda also noted that for anyone who visited the Barak Valley today, it quickly became clear that the local people feel a greater psychological affinity towards Kolkata (the capital of the neighbouring Bengali-speaking West Bengal state) or even Bangladesh than towards Guwahati or any other parts of Assam. Thus, even 60-some years after Partition, the emotional distance between Assam's two valleys, one predominantly Assamese-speaking and the other Bengali, which was one of the more pressing causes that led to the separation of Sylhet in 1947 (discussed later in the book), remains.

In this way, over a period of about eight months, detailed interviews were carried out with both Sylheti Hindus and Muslims settled on the Indian side of the border, many of which have been incorporated in the following sections. I also used some of the available popular and historical literature to weave the overall story together, and used archival sources wherever necessary. The purpose of this research was not to write a 'complete' history of the Sylhet Partition, but rather to introduce some new and human aspects of Partition that have generally remained outside the focus of historians so far. In so doing, I hoped to add to the existing knowledge about India's Partition in general, and Partition memories in particular. It was also urgent that the voices of the witnesses of Sylhet Partition be collected without any further delay—some might even consider this in itself justifies such a study.

LEARNING ABOUT SYLHET

Sylhet, a Bengali-speaking district historically a part of East Bengal, was joined to its Assamese-speaking neighbour, Assam, in 1874 by the British, who wanted to make the latter province 'economically viable' and self-sustaining. A bustling tea-growing district on the eastern fringes of East Bengal, Sylhet was flanked by the principality of Tripura in the east and southern Assam districts in the north. Separating it from the neighbouring Assamese-speaking heartland, the Brahmaputra Valley, were the towering mountain ranges of the North Cachar and Jaintia Hills. Behind these lofty mountains nestled the two districts of what now became Assam's Surma Valley—Sylhet and Cachar—whose populations mostly spoke a dialect of Bengali popularly known as Sylheti. The total area of Sylhet district was 5,440 sq. miles, and since 1874 it was divided into five sub-divisions, each of which was divided into several *thanas* within its administrative jurisdiction: Sylhet (North & South), Habiganj, Sunamganj, Maulavibazar and Karimganj. Even a cursory glance at the history of the Surma Valley in the pre-colonial period shows that Sylhet was an integral part of Bengal in the ancient and medieval period.[12] Surma Valley's relationship with Bengal was thus cemented by ethnic, linguistic, geographical and historical affinity.[13]

For several years following 1874, the Sylhet Hindus demanded a return to the culturally similar and more 'advanced' Bengal; the Sylhet Muslims, on the other hand, preferred to stay back in Assam, where its leaders believed that with their big numbers, they could help Assam's minority Muslim community develop a more powerful political voice. The indigenous Assamese too were in favour of the separation of Sylhet from Assam for the entire period 1874-1947, as the English-eduated Sylheti Hindu *bhadralok* were seen not only as competitors for jobs but as a cultural threat over an economically weak Assamese middle class which had been trying to come into its own under the aegis of British colonialism since 1826. Ironically, when the opportunity for a return to East Bengal (later East Pakistan) came in 1947, the Sylheti Hindus reversed their earlier position and demanded to stay back in Assam, while a considerable section of Sylheti Muslims also in a *volte-face* now wanted to separate. In the Referendum, a total of 239,619 votes were cast for joining

East Pakistan, and 184,041 for remaining in Assam/ India. Following this outcome, most of the Sylhet district, barring a small Hindu pocket contiguous to Assam, was ceded to East Pakistan.

Over the next three years (1947-50), a number of Sylheti Hindus from the ceded parts of Sylhet district began to migrate to the Indian north-east, particularly to the more familiar parts of southern Assam that had been continguous to Sylhet and with which they had shared economic and social relations since 1874. As more and more migrants chose to settle here, there gradually emerged a de-territorialized Sylheti identity in Assam, and Sylhetis began to form pockets of minority groups in north-east India—despite considerable local opposition to refugee settlement—contributing to powerful identity politics during the postcolonial years. In spite of being faced with assimilative drives and the loss of a firm territorialized identity, Sylhet and 'Sylheti-ness' today continue to live on in many social, cultural and political forms, particularly in Assam, which is home to the largest Sylheti settlement in India.

In what important way was the Sylhet Partition different from that in Punjab or Bengal? Let me first offer three quick examples. Mojammil Ali

Laskar, an old resident of Cachar, an area where the Sylhet Hindu population was crowding into in the aftermath of the Referendum, provides a personal account of the population displacement and role of rumour in creating and continuing an atmosphere of fear and uncertainty in the Hindu pockets of Sylhet, leading them to migrate to the Assamese side of the border. He writes:

> One day you would hear that hundreds of Hindu villages have been burnt somewhere in Sylhet. . . . The next day you would hear that Muslim mobs have entered a Dacca-bound train and killed every single Hindu passenger. . . . There was no way to verify if these stories were true.[14]

Laskar goes on to write that later, whenever he asked his refugee friends whether they had personally faced any violence, or had been witness to any such incidents, they would say they had not. None of them had lost property or money. Later on, 'they returned to Sylhet to sell off their properties, lamenting that they had not got the price that they had hoped for'.[15]

I illustrate my point with another account, which was narrated to me by Bijoy Kumar Das, a leading figure in the East Bengal refugee rehabilitation in Assam, during the course of fieldwork for a research project supported by the University Grants Commission, India. Mr Das was speaking about the arrival in Gauhati (now Guwahati) of some Sylheti 'optees':

> these optees came to Assam like tourists, camera in hand, merrily clicking pictures, as if on a holiday. I remember one incident . . . in Gauhati when some of these optees even got beaten up by the local people for their snobbery.

A third well-known example is Suhasini Das's *Sylhet Diary*, in which she describes the situation in Sylhet immediately after the results of the Referendum were announced. Published in Jashodhara Bagchi and Subhoranjan Dasgupta's book *The Trauma and the Triumph*, the excerpt opens on the day after the Referendum result was declared, and provides an account of the happenings in Sylhet until 31 January 1948. In despair and desolation, Das watches the exodus of Hindus from Sylhet, and describes the 'tension' and the 'mental agony which the Hindus suffered at this time',[16] and even refers to some 'miscreants' who seemed to be looting homes. But towards the end of the extract, she admits that 'although no major mishap had befallen people here [in Sylhet], they were still tense and anxious'.[17]

There are at least three points that make these comments particularly interesting. First, none of the scholarly or popular works on Sylhet that I have quoted above, or have read, contained accounts of major communal violence in Sylhet during or after the Referendum. This is quite in contrast with the literature, academic and popular, on the Partition in Punjab and Bengal, replete as they are with accounts of mindless (or calculated) communal violence, betrayals, forceful removal from homes, rape, abduction, etc. I can also provide supporting evidence in the form of informal discussions with many Sylheti elders and family members, among whom I have lived most of my life. Almost nobody has been able to provide me with concrete details of communal violence in Sylhet before, during or after the Referendum, although they have made frequent references to communal tensions, fears, psychological pressure and widespread rumours of violence. Admittedly, certain studies of the Bengal Partition too have pointed out that some migration was caused by the perception of threat rather than by actual violence, and that some such movement was also caused by economic dislocations that made older patterns of livelihood untenable. But references to sporadic violence in these studies still seem to be inevitable.

Second, a significant section of Sylhetis who migrated to Assam/India soon after the Referendum (1947-50) were from the middle class, a few of them English-educated 'optees',[18] a category of Partition migrants that has not yet been adequately explored by historians. Rahman and Van Schendel have pointed out that, generally, optees did not face serious problems beyond the initial inconvenience and disappointments inherent in their experience.[19] The case of Assam, however, was more complicated, where a 70-year old economic competition—which had its roots in the colonial imposition of Bengali as the official language, and subsequently in the numerical domination of the English-educated Sylhetis in the jobs and services of colonial Assam since 1874—complicated the situation of Sylheti-speaking optees when they returned to Assam post-Partition and continued to dominate the same old services as before (discussed later in this book). 'The problem of refugee influx, inbuilt within Partition proposal itself, threatened to neutralize the gains achieved by the ouster of Sylhet', writes Sujit Chaudhuri,[20] an eminent historian of Assam.

In other words, Chaudhuri suggests that the Assam government had conceded to the separation of Sylhet in the hope that it would reduce the dominance of Sylheti Hindus in Assam's economy. However, he notes that the lopping-off of most parts of Sylhet from Assam did not cut-off the Sylheti Hindu presence and competition in the various sectors of Assam's economy as large numbers of them (not just optees alone) returned to Assam following Partition and, to an extent, their grip over certain jobs and professions remained. According to one account, out of the 1,800 Assam government officers serving in Sylhet who opted to serve in India, all of those who spoke Assamese were re-instated in Assam, while many others were either discharged on gratuity or premature pension or kept on a temporary basis as juniors to their own former juniors.[21] Another optee believed that it was mostly those in the education service who found, upon arrival in Assam, that there were 'no vacancies'.[22] According to him and several other interviewees, my grandfather was one of the luckier ones, those who received their transfer orders by 14 August 1947 and were immediately reinstated in Assam. Indeed, in the manner typical of the Sylheti *bhadralok*, my father repeatedly denied that our family suffered in any way due to the relocation except lose the large ancestral home in Sylhet, and often regaled my brother and I with stories of how popular my grandfather had been as a police officer, and how the British *sahibs* had admired him for his bravery and outspokenness.

A third point is the presence of a wide gap between the personal and official histories of Sylhet. In fact, while the Sylhet Partition still remains a very live issue among Sylhetis settled around India, 'mainstream' Partition history continues to be silent on the topic. For instance, a purely academic exercise of looking up the word *Sylhet* in some of the more recent and authoritative works on Partition provided me with little information beyond a sentence or two. Some Sylheti bloggers from Bangladesh were surprised to know that 'there are Sylhetis in India as well'.[23] Parents of marriageable Indian Sylheti girls still make claims on matrimonial websites that 'we follow a traditional lifestyle basically of the value of Sylhet'.[24] Some parents even go so far as to claim sixty-odd years after Partition that 'our native place is Sylhet'.[25] Recently I found a particularly interesting comment on the Internet from a D.Phil scholar of Sylheti Hindu origin, one that expressed his yearning for a long lost homeland:

I am a Sylheti from India. I am longing for some pictures of Sylhet. That's where my ancestors hail from. We migrated to Assam in India and ever since I could never go back to Sylhet. Could you please send me some pictures of Sylhet? I am dying to see them. It will be a great help.[26]

Thus, even today Sylhet lives on in innumerable ways in the lives of tens of thousands of Indians.[27] In recent years, however, the term *Sylheti* has been used almost exclusively to refer to Bangladeshi Muslim Sylhetis. An interesting explanation for this is offered by Sanjib Baruah, who writes, 'by and large the population of Sylhet were by then [around 1926] incorporated into the powerful Calcutta-centred nationalism of Bengal and thought of themselves as Bengali . . . in this usage it probably overlapped with the Hindu-Muslim cleavage.'[28] This makes the task of locating the Hindu 'Sylheti' in India after Partition more interesting, as the identity seems to have disappeared in the late colonial era and, according to, Sukalpa Bhattacharjee, re-emerged in the Barak Valley in Assam in the post-colonial era, caught in a 'in-between' of real and imagined identity.[29]

Another comment on the Internet spells out, in a simple yet forceful manner, the Sylheti 'paradox' of remembering and forgetting its own history:

The greatest paradox is that we being such a home-loving community, such rooted to our soil, such grounded with the ethos of the place but such deep, such unbelievable forgetfulness. Such a great lapse of memory, such wonderful epilepsy cannot be explained unless we take into consideration the fact this forgetfulness might have been one of the strongest factor of our survival, physically as well as culturally, it evades all explanations. None of our literature, none of our later stories speak about this cultural discontinuity and this silence, this inexplicable silence may be more resonating than a lingering sadness, orchestrated in prose, poetry or music.[30]

This is not the only way in which Sylhet is relived in postcolonial Assam, however. Sujit Chaudhuri has argued that one of the biggest problems dogging post-colonial Assam, the 30-year old 'foreigners' problem' (undocumented migration from Bangladesh since 1971) for instance, owes itself to the unfinished business of India's Partition. Sujit Chaudhuri argues that Partition has been 'inextricably intertwined with the Assamese quest for attaining a homogeneous territory', and that the post-colonial politics constructed around the 'foreigner issue ... projected as a core question associated with the survival of the Assamese nationality, has drawn its entire rationale from Partition.'[31] In other words,

Chaudhuri is suggesting that had there been no Partition, there may have been no 'foreigner issue in Assam'.[32] It is, of course, true that much of the tenor of the post-colonial Assamese politics, particularly until the late 1980s, had been to secure Assam's identity as an 'Assamese' cultural space. During this period, some of the unwitting targets of Assam's assimilative drives have been the population of East Bengal origin, including Sylhet; thus, the legacy of the pre-Partition politics of language continues to lurk behind even the post-1947 Assam-born children of Sylhetis.

The 1947 Sylhet Referendum and Partition was the defining moment of the Indian Sylheti identity for three main reasons. First, it marked the splintering of the Sylheti identity into at least two nationalities: the Bangladeshi and the Indian Sylheti. As noted earlier, the Bangladeshi Sylheti identity has come to be widely recognized as the 'primary' Sylheti identity (as a simple google search will demonstrate), one associated with Muslims from Sylhet division of modern Bangladesh. The Indian Sylheti identity which is associated primarily with Hindus from the retained parts of erstwhile Sylhet district, on the other hand, is little understood or recognized outside of eastern India.

Second, the Referendum and Partition were collectively the 'un-hinging' moment of Indian Sylheti history, when the territory was separated from colonial India and became part of a new and different country. On the other hand, it can also be thought of as the 'hinging' moment of Indian Sylheti history, when the futures of large numbers of Sylhetis living on that territory became entwined with the history of the newly independent India.

Third, this was the beginning of a 'de-territor-ialized' Sylheti identity in India, when the official name of the province was retained solely by East Pakistan, unlike Punjab or Bengal whose names were retained in independent India. The part of Sylhet that stayed back within India, on the other hand, was subsumed within Assam's Cachar district, and thereafter disappeared forever from the map of India. In later years, while Indian Sylhetis associated themselves territorially with Karimganj (the retained part of erstwhile Sylhet) or Silchar in Assam, or simply within Assam generally, their imagined identity remained tied to the distant homeland in Sylhet, even though this was now part of a different country. In this way, many 'new deterritorialized Sylhets', standing uncertainly between a real and imagined identity, were recreated in multiple parts of the Indian north-east and, over time, 'Sylheti-ness' was regularly reproduced in these areas.

LOSS OF THE SYLHETI MEMORY

During and after Partition, tales of atrocities were used as propaganda by both Hindu and Muslim communities in India. Later, such stories were used by both to justify and valorize their respective roles during Partition, which often alternated between being perpetrators and victims of violence. The postcolonial political mood of Assam, however, did not generally encourage public articulations of the history of Sylhet Referendum and Partition; and Sylhetis, especially those who relocated in the Assamese-majority Brahmaputra Valley, developed new ways of safekeeping their memories—storing them largely in the private realm, while adopting strategies of 'forgetting' in public.

This was particularly the case after the start of the Assam Movement (1979-85), which was ostensibly organized around the detection and deportation of undocumented Bangladeshi immigrants, but which often confused the latter with *bohiragoto* or Indian outsiders, who were seen as a 'threat to the Asamiya [Assamese] identity'.[33] It was only in intimate locations (homes, among friends and family) that such stories were shared, and even then only occasionally. Remembering in the public sphere was inevitably political, after all; the question of what could or should be remembered and said became intimately tied to the issue of political allegiance of a minority community.

Over time, however, community relationships in Assam evolved and thawed. This was particularly brought about with the ebbing of the Assam Movement, the overtaking of the Bohiragoto issue by undocumented migration from Bangladesh, as well as the onslaught of the forces of religious fundamentalism and globalization which brought Assam face-to-face with many new and diverse socio-political challenges as the rest of India. Nonetheless, the voices of Sylheti Hindus in the Brahmaputra Valley for the most part remained silent with regard to their own unique history, in spite of the existence of a reasonably articulate and culturally active, though small, middle class. There could be many reasons for this. The generation that had directly and personally experienced Partition is now much older and no longer active in public life. Many of this generation continue to live 'in exile' like many other diasporas around the world, often nurturing a desire, not to return, but to lament, valorize and re-create the lost homeland. The Assam-born younger generation, on the other hand, has been partly pragmatic, partly assimilated within the surrounding Assamese society, and also partly globalized—thus making it increasingly difficult for them to remain connected to a distant past. This generation, like me, is now largely bi-lingual and is easily able to negotiate its identity between being 'Assamese' and 'Sylheti'. In fact, the post-1947 born generation in the Brahmaputra Valley often refers to its evolving identity as *Assam-er Bangali* (Bengalis of Assam) indicating that their historical experience is closely tied to Assam, and this is what makes their position *vis-à-vis* other Bengalis (in West Bengal and other parts of India) different. The overlapping histories of Sylhet and Assam is an important acculturating factor, as is the apparent closeness of the Sylheti and Assamese languages. Ironically, however, though the 'new-ness' of the 'new land' is not so apparent to the generation that was born in independent India, yet the politics of identity in post-colonial Assam has kept them informed of their 'migrant' status from time to time.

Again, no large-scale oral-history projects were undertaken to capture Sylheti Hindu memories of Partition, and few historians outside Assam attempted to document this important chapter of Indian history. Thus, the stories of the Sylhet Referendum and Partition were largely left out of the slew of new ethnographies on Partition memories undertaken by eminent scholars since the 1980s. Historical records are still hard to come by, and oral accounts have to be collected in person through fieldwork in far-flung areas, mostly in north-east India. But what is particularly critical for the future of this population is that many younger Sylheti Hindus born in the Brahmaputra Valley ten or fifteen years after the Referendum and Partition have little knowledge of their own unique history.

FORGETTING SYLHET

This issue of remembering and forgetting came into sharp focus when I started work on the current study. Was it worth digging out the painful memories that had been long forgotten, even purposefully buried? On the other hand, as an Assam-born post-1947 Sylheti myself, I also realized the importance of remembering, and documenting whatever bits of the history that I could salvage even sixty years afterwards. As introduced earlier, as a historian I viewed the Sylhet Referendum and Partition as the moment when Sylheti history was severed from that of India and was irrevocably tied to East Pakistan (later Bangladesh). Locating this moment and inscribing it into the pages of Indian history would legitimize the community's subsequent relocation into post-colonial India, and clearly display its long association with the region.

Why the Partition of Sylhet has not received adequate attention of historians, particularly at a time when Partition historiography is being regularly critiqued and re-written in the light of newer and unconventional sources, remains a matter of speculation. One reason could be that East Pakistan itself had an unexpectedly short history of only twenty-six years, at the end of which it became a new country, Bangladesh, which in turn began a new chapter in that country's history. Also, the subsequent acceleration of population displacement in Bangladesh perhaps lessened the significance of the Sylhet Partition migration, which took place with comparatively little physical violence compared to that during the Liberation War of 1971. Further, the oral or literary voices of Sylheti Partition migrants (both Hindus and Muslims) did not capture the popular or scholarly imagination to the same extent as those from Punjab or Bengal, where Partition unfolded with a much higher scale of violence. In her article 'Uprooted and Divided', Meghna Guhathakurta points out that

> memories of 1947 or Partition have often been superseded by memories of 1971, or movements, which led to 1971 because in the quest for a Bengali identity many Bengali Muslims had to rethink their positions. Thus when memories of Partition are revived, they are either blocked or coloured by memories of 1971.[34]

One might be tempted to ask why the memories of 1947, were 'buried' as it were by the powerful outpourings of 1971 memories. Is it only natural that more recent memories replace the older memories? Perhaps the answer can be found in the politics of memory by which I mean a pragmatic use of the 1971 memories as it better suited the identity of postcolonial Bangladesh than that of 1947. The

Sylhet Partition migration has therefore ended up becoming a story (or memory) of Indian Hindus alone, and remains marginalized even in the national narratives of Bangladesh. This is not to suggest, however, that East Bengal/Bangladesh was not impacted by post-Partition population displacement. David Ludden points out that, in the wake of Partition, some 100,000 Muslim Bengalis moved out of Assam into Sylhet's Haor basin, where open land was available. Sylhet's population growth was most dramatic in areas nearest Meghalaya and Tripura, where migration produced completely new localities populated entirely by immigrants.[35]

Another explanation could be that the Sylhet Partition was embedded in the discourse of the politics of language in Assam, of which Sylhet was a part for 73 years until 1947. Since Sylhet's incorporation into the predominantly Assamese-speaking province for the 'administrative convenience' of the Raj, there was an effort made by both Sylhetis and the Assamese to reverse the administrative decision, but to no avail. In fact, scholars like Amalendu Guha, Sujit Chaudhuri, Monirul Hussain, Sanjib Baruah, etc., have pointed out that one of the issues around which nineteenth-century Assamese nationalism developed was the separation of the Bengali-speaking and Muslim-majority Sylhet, the incorporation of which was seen as a threat to the survival of the Assamese race. Thus, in 1947 the Assamese political elite were relieved to have the unwelcome Bengali Muslim-dominated area finally ceded to Pakistan, as Sujit Chaudhuri argues in his article 'A Godsent Opportunity'. In post-colonial years there was little interest among local historians or novelists writing in Assamese or Bengali (with the notable exceptions of Syed Abdul Malik and Homen Bargohain) to document the migration from East Bengal to Assam; but even Malik and Bargohain did not specifically address the issue of post-Partition Sylheti migration in their brilliant works of fiction.

Sylhet in turn produced few of its own Partition historians, filmmakers or creative writers who could tell its story to the rest of the country, and the sporadic works that did come out failed to capture the imagination of the rest of India. In her path-breaking work *The Other Side of Silence*, Urvashi Butalia admits that 'a major lacuna' of her work was that she had not 'looked at the east', mainly because she did not 'have the language' to do so. Subhoranjan Dasgupta and Jasodhara Bagchi's edited book on Partition in the east tried to address this gap and yet, besides the excerpts from Suhasini Das's *Partition Diary*, there is little else on Sylhet. Likewise, Gyanendra Pandey's well-known book *Remembering Partition* contained only two references to Sylhet, but neither in relation to the Referendum or the Partition displacement. A survey of several well-known Partition historiographies also provide painfully little material on the Sylhet Referendum or Partition.

At the time of writing this book, therefore, there exist very few scholarly works on the Sylhet Partition, numbering eight to ten at the most (mostly journal articles), written by Assam's historians, and a book in English on the impact of Partition in Bengal and Assam which devotes a few chapters to the Sylhet Referendum and Partition. Besides these, I discovered a smattering of memoirs and autobiographies published in Cachar (Assam's predominantly Sylheti/Bengali-speaking Barak Valley)[36] or Kolkata, penned by Sylheti Hindus mostly belonging to the Partition generation; there are also a few internet blogs maintained by younger Sylhetis. Thus, if one were to leave out the memories of the Partition eyewitnesses, there exists very little material on which to base a popular history of Sylhet Partition today. On the other hand, one can hardly forget the short stories of Saadat Hasan Manto, which brought readers face to face with the sordid human tragedy of Partition in Punjab. Without a reference to Manto's works, no study on India's Partition is complete today—and it is unfortunate that Sylhet did not produce its own Manto.

DISCOURSES ON THE SYLHET PARTITION

Though the existing research is still thin, significant contributions to the understanding of Sylhet Partition have been made by scholars like Amalendu Guha, Jayanta Bhushan Bhattacharjee, Bidyut Chakrabarty, Sanjib Baruah and Sujit Chaudhuri. These studies can be taken as the founding basis of a more detailed history of both the Sylhet Referendum and Partition. Guha, arguably Assam's best-known historian, deals with the issue of Sylhet in his iconic book *Planter Raj to Swaraj: Freedom and Electoral Politics in Assam, 1826-1947*, in which he writes that the incorporation of Sylhet into the Chief Commissionership of Assam on 12 September 1874 created two valley-based identities: the Brahmaputra Valley (Assam proper), with its mostly Hindu and

Assamese-speaking population, and the Surma Valley (Sylhet and Cachar), with a Muslim majority and Bengali-speaking population. The illogicality of such a colonial decision is clear when Guha terms Assam and Sylhet as 'strange bedfellows'. In addition, since the jobs and membership of elected local bodies were decided along valley lines, this slowly gave rise to what Guha calls 'valley-jealousy' as the Surma Valley with its early start in English education grabbed a disproportionate share of Assam's jobs. What was originally an economic competition between the two valleys soon manifested itself in the politics of language where the native Assamese began to feel the pressure of economic competition from the Sylheti Hindus who now proliferated into the different sectors of the provincial economy. Gradually the Assamese middle class began to articulate demands for 'saving the Assamese race' which was now in danger of being swept away by the growing numbers of Bengali/Sylhetis in Assam.

When on 3 June 1947 the Mountbatten Award announced that a Referendum would be held in Sylhet to decide whether it should stay within India or join East Pakistan, however, the Sylheti Hindus, who for decades had agitated for reunion with

Bengal, now clung to Assam. The rise of communal politics in India on the eve of India's freedom had completely overturned the Hindu community's long-held stance. On the other hand, the Sylheti Muslims, who for political reasons had wanted to remain within Assam since 1874, now wanted to join East Pakistan in the changed political mood. But on the Sylhet question, Guha writes, the Assamese public opinion was understandably cold and consistent with its earlier attitude. In fact, in 1945-6 the Assam Pradesh Congress Committee's election manifesto had pledged to the electorate that the Congress party would work towards separating Sylhet from Assam.

'The Congress control of Assam administration was so "correctly" exercised that it hardly provided any advantage to the local Congress during its campaign in Sylhet to win the Referendum,' writes Guha. 'It was indeed a life-time's opportunity for the Assamese leadership to get rid of Sylhet and carve out a linguistically more homogeneous province.'[37]

Thus, he concludes, 'Sylhet, the golden calf, which was sacrificed in 1874 to usher in a new province [Assam], was now once more sacrificed at the altar of a new state'.[38]

The well-known historian Jayanta Bhushan Bhattacharjee argues that the inclusion of Sylhet into Assam happened at a time when 'the Assamese-Bengali conflict in Assam Valley had already assumed a breaking point'[39] over the imposition of Bengali, not Assamese, as the official language of the province. Soon afterwards, the province also experienced a growing influx of Muslim farmers from districts in East Bengal who now settled in large numbers in the Brahmaputra Valley. The rapid growth of population 'was viewed by the Assamese as a danger for the local community who could be culturally swamped and demographically outnumbered by the dominant and numerous immigrant [Bengali-speaking] community'.[40]

Thus, almost right from the time of its inclusion in Assam, the native Assamese demanded that Sylhet be returned to Bengal. Bhattacharjee also writes that, as a young man at the time of the Sylhet Referendum, former Education Minister Triguna Sen had believed that 'the transfer of Sylhet to Pakistan had already been secretly decided upon and accepted by the Congress High Command and also by many in the Assam Congress to reduce the Bengali element in Assam's population' before the Referendum took place.[41]

In 'A Godsent Opportunity', Sujit Chaudhuri likewise explains that the principal reason behind the transfer of Sylhet was a longstanding demand on the part of the indigenous Assamese, represented by the Assam Pradesh Congress Committee.[42] Chaudhuri argues that the separation of Sylhet, following a referendum, had its origin in what can be termed a long-cherished quest of the Assamese—carving out a homogeneous province for themselves. The Assamese, he writes, perceived the Partition of 1947 as a 'Godsent opportunity' to attain that role, as Sylhet was seen as 'an ulcer hindering the emergence of a unilingual Assam'.[43]

Political scientist Bidyut Chakrabarty's major contribution to the study of the Sylhet Partition is a book titled,[44] *The Partition of Bengal and Assam, 1932-47: Contour of Freedom.* In this thoroughly researched work, Chakrabarty provides an account of the circumstances leading to the Referendum, the details of the Referendum itself and its consequences. Based primarily on little-known archival sources, *The Partition of Bengal and Assam* for the first time presents many little-known details of this controversial chapter of India's Partition. This study too situates the question of the Sylhet Referendum and Partition within the broader questions of the politics of language (Assamese-Bengali) and communalism (Hindu-Muslim), and raises questions about the ways in which the Referendum was hurriedly pushed through at very short notice.

While the historians discussed here appear to be in agreement in their interpretation of the circumstances leading to the Sylhet Referendum and Partition, a different interpretation is offered by Sanjib Baruah in his book *India Against Itself: The Politics of Nationality in Assam.* Here, Baruah suggests that the surprise inclusion of the Bengali-speaking Sylhet into the Assamese-speaking Assam in 1874 was a result of colonial decisions based on the notion that 'Assam was an extension of Bengal'. The primary goal of making Assam into a new administrative entity was to find an inexpensive and effective way to administer the area, and thus considerations of historical or cultural continuity were not in the minds of colonial officers. While the British went on to introduce Bengali as the official language of the new province (considering Assamese as an offshoot of Bengali), the Assamese public intellectuals argued that they were a distinctive people with a distinctive language and culture, writes Baruah.

Neither the Assamese intellectuals nor the Assamese members of the elected and representative bodies were powerful or organized enough to pressure the British into reconsidering this decision, however, other than to make loud demands from time to time for the separation of Sylhet from Assam. Soon enough, with their prior English-language education and experience in British administrative services in Bengal, the Sylhetis began to dominate the government and service sectors in Assam, thus causing an acute sense of relative deprivation among the local Assamese. In turn, this gave rise to a competition between the Assamese and Bengali communities in Assam, one that continued well into the post-colonial period. The controversial Sylhet question, Baruah writes, came to an end only with its cession to East Pakistan in 1947.[45]

PEOPLE-TALK ABOUT SYLHET

It was during my fieldwork in 2000-1 and again in 2007-8 in Assam's Cachar district that I found some popular literature written in Bengali, mostly memoirs, that offered deeply personal perspectives on Sylhet Partition. Over the years I also discovered a number of websites and blogs maintained by Sylhetis in which they continue to discuss issues of Sylheti identity in independent India in interestingly crafted out discussions and sometimes, scholarly articles. Written by a generation of Sylheti Hindus who, for the most part, had personally experienced the impact of Partition, this body of popular literature established a predominant motif of the Referendum being manipulated: first by political leaders from both the Indian National Congress and the Muslim League and their supporters, and second by forces from outside of Sylhet. At first, most of these writings seem typical of Partition writings on Punjab and Bengal, or what Ishtiaq Ahmed (who has worked extensively on Punjab Partition memories) calls painting 'rose-tinted portrayals of communal harmony'[46] in pre-Partition Sylhet. Most begin by suggesting an idyllic past when Hindus and Muslims lived in peace, until Partition changed everything. For instance, Binapani Roy of erstwhile Sylhet district recalled,

> Our village had more Hindus than Muslims. The Hindus owned the land, the Muslims tilled it. Relations between

the communities were quite acceptable. But as soon as the Referendum results came out, panic spread among the Hindus. Muslims went around saying 'Let us first get Pakistan; we shall then get even with the Hindus'.[47]

Some writers spoke of Hindu-Muslim *shampriti* (good relations) in Sylhet, the land of 'Shah Jalal and Sri Chaitanya'. Krishna Kumar Palchoudhury admitted even when communalism reared its ugly head, during the latter part of British rule, 'perhaps the air in Sylhet was slightly polluted' but this was due only to 'outside interference'.[48] He went on to point out that 'Sylhetis treat each other as brothers . . . though they may not be related, the dhoti and lungi-wearing Sylhetis called themselves district brothers [*jela-tto bhai*].'[49] Similarly, barely two weeks after the Referendum, Suhasini Das wrote of the 'beautiful relationship between Hindus and Muslims' of Sylhet, which has been 'deteriorating day by day'.[50]

Another Sylheti, who is now settled in London, reminisced on the internet,

> Almost 80% of houses (except our Bari) near our area used to be Hindu houses. These were still called Madhab Bari, Kamar Bari, Palor Bari, Mazon Bari, Nath Bari, Dhuli Bari, Huna ramor chowk, Shonamonir Bari . . . many more.

. . . I remember Deepak, Deepali, Hirendra, Tutul, Mani etc. used to come to our house to collect Bel phool for their pooja. It was such a nice environment. Then came this virulent xenophobia that gradually vanished everything. People became greedy and narrow-minded.[51]

These writers generally avoid explaining the reasons that changed the cordial relationship between Hindus and Muslims. They do not blame the Sylheti Muslims for being the prime perpetrators of communalism; instead, their writings seem to suggest that this community was swayed towards communalism by jingoistic politicians, and that the main responsibility for Sylhet's Partition lay with the *desher netara*, the leaders of the country. In his Bengali-language book *Srihatter Sreshtho Santanera* (Famous Children of Sylhet), Bijan Bihari Purkayastha speaks of a *marmantik bedona* (terrible pain) in his heart due to the 'game' of *kutil rajniti* (nefarious politics) that was successfully played out by politicians in Sylhet at the time of Partition.[52] These writers also seem to deny the presence of fissures within the Sylheti community and social relations, instead attempt to locate the cause of the disruption of social harmony from outside the society or circle of friends. Even during interviews, most Sylheti Hindus were unable or did not want to explain who or what was the real cause behind this disruption of the Sylheti community on the eve of Partition. The answers to such questions typically varied from *Kita je hoiya gelo!* (I don't know what happened!), followed by a long, deep sigh or a listless *Jaani na kemne eto-shob hoiya gelo* (I don't know how all this happened).

Apparent in these writings, however, is a lingering sense of political victimization within the community, even so many years after Partition. While it is not so difficult to understand why the Sylheti Hindus saw themselves as victims of a communal politics in 1947, a question that nonetheless must be asked is why being Sylheti was seen as a factor for their victimization. Why, in their opinion, did the Indian National Congress not do enough, before and during the Referendum, to keep Sylhet in Assam? Sylheti writers point out how life in Sylhet was abruptly disrupted by the intervention of communal politics and politicians from 'outside the district', and suggest that the Referendum results were manipulated, that there was political conspiracy involved, and that Sylhet was 'sacrificed' to East Pakistan in 1947.

While recalling the way that the Referendum was conducted, some writers use expressions such as *bishuddha chakranta* (clear conspiracy), *onyaye* (injustice), *goondamee* (hooliganism), etc. Many have spoken of the disenfranchisement of the 150,000 non-Muslim tea-garden labourers during the Referendum—which, they felt, could have been crucial in changing the final verdict of the Referendum. One writer complained that, at the time of the Referendum, ferries were virtually closed in the Hindu areas, ostensibly in an attempt to keep members of these communities from casting their votes. Considering that the voting was organized in the monsoon months of July, during which large parts of East Bengal generally remained flooded, it was nearly impossible to travel within Sylhet without using the ferry service. A Congress volunteer who was active during the Referendum wrote that there were allegations that the Muslim superintendent of the Government Press of Assam (where the ballot papers were printed) printed false papers, issuing these to the members of the Muslim League to increase the number of ballots cast. Many such charges and counter-charges were made by party workers of both the Congress and the Muslim League.

These accounts bring us to a 'twist' in the Partition plot. It is commonly held that the Indian National

Congress had stood firmly against the idea of Partition, but ultimately could do little to stop it from happening. Suhasini Das, however, writes, 'They [the people of Sylhet] started abusing the Congress Party too. They were holding the Party responsible for this tension. Why did they agree to a popular vote? Why didn't they stop this?'[53] Rabindranath Aditya, a Congress leader of Sylhet who was active during the Referendum, likewise wrote:

> The Assam leadership, too eager to get rid of Sylhet with a view to carving out a homogeneous province arranged little protection of minorities of Sylhet in the free exercise of their united franchise. When the results of the Referendum were declared, there was a subdued sense of relief in the Assam Valley as the majority of the votes were cast in favour of Pakistan.[54]

In his book *Pak-Bharoter Ruprekha* (The Contours of India and Pakistan), on the other hand, Prabhash Chandra Lahiri argues that the erstwhile Congress party home minister of Assam, Basanta Kumar Das of Sylhet, did not do enough to stop the Partition of the area. As early as 1928, Das had moved an amendment suggesting that a Referendum be arranged to 'ascertain the views of all *chowkidari* (landowners) and municipal rate-payers of Sylhet and Cachar regarding the transfer question', though the amendment was rejected by 29 to 12 votes at the time.[55] Lahiri recalls a discussion that allegedly took place between him and Das, during which the latter admitted, 'I should have tendered my resignation at that time [of the Referendum]. I am paying the price for not doing that by living in Pakistan today.' Das had stayed back after Partition, and had gone on to become the finance minister of East Pakistan and a central minister in the cabinet. The author adds,

> Das indeed paid the ultimate price. A man, who possessed more than 50 bighas of land in Sylhet, could not breathe his last in the home of his ancestors. During the regime of Ayub Khan, he had to flee to Calcutta where he passed away in his son-in-law's rented house.[56]

This was later to become a fairly common refrain in the writings of some other authors. Take the well-known Sylheti author Amitava Chowdhuri, for instance, whose words, if loosely translated from Bengali, would mean that Basanta Kumar Das 'simply did not bother'.[57]

The central point made by the writers has to do with the politics of language arising out of what was essentially an economic disparity between the Assamese and Bengalis in Assam. This was a result of the domination of the Bengali-speaking Sylheti 'babus' (originally an honorific, it became a name for English-educated clerks) in the government and other sectors of employment, the imposition by the British government of the Bengali language as the official language of Assam at a time when it was being spoken only by a small but powerful minority, and the post-1874 inclusion of Sylhet and Cachar as well as large-scale migration of Muslim peasants from East Bengal districts which, taken together, unexpectedly increased the numbers of Bengali-speaking population in Assam. Yet this critical point is hardly ever addressed in popular writings. These writings do not make references to either the 'valley jealousy' discussed earlier, or the desire for the politicians of Assam to carve out a linguistically homogeneous state for themselves in independent India. In fact, these works deal with the actual moment of Partition rather than provide long-term causes or analysis. More specifically, while the writers do refer to 'Congress politics' and do put some blame on the politicians, it is never made particularly clear as to what the politicians' agenda was. One is left to figure out whether these political actors, who were seen to be conspiring against the people of Sylhet, were inspired by communalism (Hindu-Muslim) or the politics of language (Assamese-Bengali), or both.

In general, though, both the popular and historical works on the Sylhet Referendum and Partition construct two entities as the 'other', who thereafter are held responsible for not doing enough in order to prevent the area's partition. The first was the Assam Pradesh Congress Committee, whose leaders, for a long time, had been vocal in demanding Sylhet's separation. Both popular and historical writings repeatedly point to a 'disinterest' on the part of the Assam Pradesh Congress Committee to exert itself in keeping Sylhet, either before or during the Referendum. The Premier of Assam, and the leader of the Assam Congress Gopinath Bardoloi himself, however, provides a clue into his role during the Referendum in his own word. Bardoloi had visited Mahatma Gandhi soon after the Boundary Commission (for Bengal, and later Sylhet) was set up as he was worried over rumours that there was a conspiracy to include Goalpara, Cachar and some other parts of Assam into East Pakistan.

The meeting that he had with Mahatma Gandhi over this issue is vividly described by Bardoloi himself. As he narrated his own fears and worries, the

Mahatma asked him why then in the first place had Bardoloi agreed to the Referendum. When Bardoloi answered that he had played no role in it, Gandhi retorted that nothing can happen in a province without the Premier's knowledge. 'I then told him all I knew', wrote Bardoloi.

> . . . how Lord Mountbatten at a lunch to which I was invited, said that he presumed that I was indifferent about Sylhet going to Pakistan. I told him, however, that while it was true that a large number of the people in Assam Valley wanted Sylhet to be separated and at one time even the Hindus of Sylhet wanted the same, the Congressmen of both the places wanted to live together as they fought a common fight together for ten long years under my leadership for weal or woe. I told him also how Lord Mountbatten met the leader of Sylhet, the then Home Minister of our cabinet (Sri Basanta Kumar Das), the same evening at a garden party and how the latter agreed to the Referendum and how the Working Committee of Congress endorsed it. I then put to him,—How can I fight the working Committee?[58]

Bidyut Chakrabarty apportions some of the responsibility to Jawaharlal Nehru, who, 'despite his misgivings about the outcome of the Referendum due to the reported intimidation of the Muslim National Guards . . . accepted the [Referendum] verdict.'[59] As discussed above, some others partly hold Basanta Kumar Das responsible for not doing enough in this regard, though Makhan Lal Kar, a volunteer during the Referendum, stated that Das was informally divested of his portfolio on the eve of the vote, and that therefore he could do very little to influence the organization or outcome of the Referendum.[60] Das, he wrote, 'stuck to office without power'.[61] In fact, Kar also mentioned that Das had made two revealing statements on the eve of the Referendum. He said:

> there was promise that the Referendum would be conducted under the military supervision with the help of the provincial police. The provincial government have already exhausted all their police and other resources and it was the inadequacy of the military deployed for the purpose that had made it impossible to conduct the referendum in a peaceful atmosphere.[62]

Second, Das also pointed out that there was 'organized hooliganism in different parts of the [Sylhet] district and that the police and the army-men deployed were not enough to deal with the situation'.[63] But the Assam governor, Sir Akbar Hydari, did not take his comments seriously, and even informed the national-level Congress leaders that Das' views were not borne out by facts on the ground. In his book in Bengali, *Swadhinata Andolon-e Srihatta* (Sylhet during the Freedom Movement) B.B. Purakayastha wrote that since the national leadership of the Indian National Congress had accepted the verdict of a Referendum, the local-level Congress leaders also demonstrated an enthusiastic approach. Therefore, in spite of being the home minister, Basanta Kumar Das remained only a 'helpless witness of circumstances'.[64]

The second entity that some of the writers held responsible was the Bengal Muslim League, its leaders and workers, with many popular works having highlighted its organizational strength and dedication to win the Referendum at any cost. The Congress did not seem to have zealously pursued the campaign against the inclusion of Sylhet in East Pakistan, while the Muslim League left no stone unturned to mobilize the district's Muslims in its favour.[65]

During interviews I was repeatedly informed that the only politician from the Brahmaputra Valley to personally visit Sylhet and actively canvass for the retention of the area within India was the popular Assamese politician Rohini Kumar Chowdhury. Many Sylheti Hindus I interviewed spoke of his 'liberal attitude' in glowing terms. However, it was widely believed that no other Congress leader, at either the national or provincial level, Hindu or Muslim, visited or campaigned at the Referendum.

This discussion throws open two possibilities for consideration in Partition studies as a whole. First, that the Indian National Congress during the 1940s did not really have a unified stand on the issue of Partition. It is generally believed that the Congress was in favour of retaining Sylhet in India, and that the Muslim League was in favour of its Partition on the basis of religion. The Sylhet experience, however, suggests that the Congress party was equally swayed by the local politics of language in Assam as by communalism, and did not pose major objections to the proposed separation of Sylhet despite allegations of mismanagement of the Referendum and demands for a second Referendum. Another reason for the Congress's acceptance of the verdict of the July Referendum despite many accusations of organizational malpractices was the time factor: in order for India to gain its independence on 15 August 1947, there was no time to organize a second Referendum though such a request was forwarded by the Sylheti Hindu leaders to the government. Third, communal politics might not have been the only factor behind Partition. As the case of Sylhet shows, the local politics of language played a crucial role in constructing and perpetuating the problem of Sylhet in the Assamese narrative since the late 1870s, which was later merged with the national politics of communalism. The 'valley jealousy' had been around for much longer than communal politics, yet during the 1940s both strands came together in the shape of the July Referendum.

NOTES

1. Pierre Nora, 'Between Memory and History: Les Lieux de Mémoire' (tr. Marc Roudebush) in Genevieve Fabre and Robert O'Meally (eds.), *History and Memory in African-American Culture,* New York, 1994.
2. Pierre Nora, 'Between Memory and History: Les Lieux de Mémoire' [1984]. *Representations* 26, Spring 1989, pp. 7-25.
3. Akoma Chiji, 'The "Trick" of Narratives: History, Memory, and Performance in Toni Morrison's Paradise', *Oral Tradition* 15(1), 2000, p. 5.
4. George Lipsitz, 'Myth, History, and Counter-Memory', in Adam J. Sorkin (ed.), *Politics and the Muse: Studies in the Politics of Recent American Literature*, Bowling Green: Bowling Green State University Press, 1989, p. 162.
5. Urvashi Butalia, *The Other Side of Silence: Voices from the Partition of India*, Durham: Duke University Press, 2000, p. 10.

6. Gertrude Himmelfarb, *The New History and the Old: Critical Essays and Reappraisals*, Cambridge, MA, and London: Harvard University Press, 1987, p. 15.
7. Butalia, op. cit., p. 10.
8. Meenakshie Verma, *Aftermath: An Oral History of Violence,* New Delhi: Penguin, 2004.
9. Ibid., p. xiii.
10. Ibid., p. xiv.
11. Note: they used the name 'Bangladesh' instead of 'Pakistan'.
12. Sanghamitra Paul Choudhury, 'Sylhet Referendum-1947', unpublished M. Phil dissertation, North-Eastern Hill University, Shillong, 1992, p. 7.
13. Ibid., pp. 7-8.
14. Mojammil Ali Laskar, *Aamar Balyo, Aamar Koishor: Cacharer Shekaal*, Silchar: no publisher, 1999.
15. Ibid., p. 176.
16. Jasodhara Bagchi and Shubhoranjan Dasgupta (eds.), *The Trauma and the Triumph: Gender and Partition in Eastern, India*, Kolkata: Stree, 2003, p. 170.
17. Ibid., p. 173.
18. Exchange of certain categories of state personnel between Pakistan and India was organized by allowing them to opt for a position in the other state. These 'optees', who arrived at the time of Partition, took the place of counterparts who travelled the other way. They took charge of tasks at all levels and in all branches of the government. Other displaced people joined the state on an individual basis. The influence of these newcomers on state formation and state policies in the three countries has, to our knowledge, never been studied, let alone compared. http://www.idpad.org/docs/Vol.%20I%20%20No.%20

1%20January-June%202003.pdf accessed on 15 June 2007.

19. Rahman and Van Schendel, 2003, op. cit., p. 564.
20. Sujit Chaudhuri, 'A "god-sent" opportunity?', *Seminar*, no. 510, February 2002.
21. Choudhury, 1954, op. cit. During fieldwork among optees, several others also supported this point.
22. Email discussion with Mihir Datta now residing in the United States. There were several other optees in his immediate family.
23. '[I] didn't realize that there was a Sylhet in India, until someone mentioned it in a topic, I was very suprised seeing as I am a Sylheti from Bangladesh and didn't realise that there [are] different types of Sylhet around the world' http://www.sylheti.com/messages/SylhetiandIndia.html 21/5/2007 accessed on 21 May 2007.
24. bmser.telugumatrimony.com/cgi-bin/viewprofile.php?idB417467 accessed on 20 May 2007.
25. bmser.bharatmatrimony.com/cgi-bin/viewprofile.php?idB258048 accessed on 20 May 2007.
26. http://lughat.blogspot.com/2006/05/sylheti-word-order.html accessed on 24 May 2007.
27. 'Today I am Homeless . . . my father died homeless . . . from 1938 my father served Indian Railways in Assam . . . we were never refugees . . . yet lost everything'. http://74.6.146.244/search/cache?eiUTF8&phomeless+sylheti&fryfp501&fp_ipMY&u/www.sylheti.com/messages/SylhetiandIndia.html&whomeless+sylheti&dLKCeuurnOp68&icp1&.intlus
28. Baruah, 1999, op. cit., p. 42.
29. Sukalpa Bhattacharjee, 'Sylheti Narratives: Memory to

Identity', in Sukalpa Bhattacharjee and Rajesh Dev (eds), *Ethno-Narratives: Identity and Experience in North East India*, New Delhi: Ansha Publishing House, 2006.

30. http://personal.vsnl.com/syhlleti/para1.htm accessed on 20 May 2007.
31. Chaudhuri, 2002, op. cit.
32. Ibid.
33. Monirul Hussain, *The Assam Movement: Class, Ideology, Identity,* New Delhi: Manak Publications, 1993, p. 101.
34. Meghna Guha Thakurta, 'Uprooted and Divided', http://www.india-seminar.com/2002/510/510%20meghna%20guha%20thakurta.htm accessed on 4 July 2008
35. David Ludden, 'Political Maps and Cultural Territories', *Himal Southasian*, http://www.sas.upenn.edu/~dludden/LuddenHIMALSylhet1.htm retrieved on 26 March 2008.
36. Assam is divided into two valleys, the Brahmaputra and the Barak, the latter before 1947 known as Surma Valley, where both Sylhet and Cachar districts were located. The former is the traditional homeland of the Assamese while the latter has large Sylheti/Bengali settlements. Since its incorporation into Assam in 1874, many Sylhetis moved to both valleys to fill up middle level government jobs. At present, the Barak Valley zealously guards its Sylheti/Bengali identity within Assam state whereas in the Brahmaputra Valley younger generations of Sylheti/Bengalis have largely integrated with Assamese language and culture. This is one of the reasons while memories of Sylhet remain alive in the Barak Valley; it is nearly forgotten in the Brahmaputra Valley.
37. Amalendu Guha, op. cit., p. 261.

38. Ibid., p. 320.
39. Jayanta Bhushan Bhattacharjee, 'Sylhet: Myth of a Referendum', *Indo-British Review: A Journal of History,* 18(1&2), 1989
40. Ibid., p. 38.
41. Ibid., p. 49.
42. Chaudhuri, 2002, op. cit.
43. Ibid.
44. Bidyut Chakrabarty, *The Partition of Bengal and Assam, 1932-47: Contour of Freedom*, London & New York: Routledge.
45. For a discussion see Baruah, op. cit., pp. 38-43.
46. Ishtiaq Ahmed, 'Forced Migration and Ethnic Cleansing in Lahore in 1947: Some First Person Accounts', in Ian Talbot and Shinder Thandi (eds), *People on the Move: Punjabi Colonial, and Post-Colonial Migration,* Karachi: Oxford University Press, 2004, p. 6.
47. Ravindranath Trivedi, 'The Legacy of the Plight of Hindus in Bangladesh, Part IV', *The Asian Tribune,* http://www.asiantribune.com/index.php? qnode/6606 retrieved on 27 December 2007.
48. Krishna Kumar Pal Choudhury, 'Sylhet, Sylhetitwa O' Sylhet-er Ahonkar', in S. Debray (ed.), *Sribhumi Srihatta: Sreehatter Samskriti Bishayak Prabandha Samkalan,* Durgapur Srihatta Sammilani, p. 1. (Translation from Bengali mine.)
49. Ibid.
50. Suhasini Das, 'Partition: A Diary', in Bagchi and Dasgupta (eds.), op. cit., p. 169.
51. Shaheen, http://personal.vsnl.com/syhlleti/barlekha.html accessed on 22 May 2007.

52. Bijan Bihari Purakayastha, *Srihatter Sreshtho Santanera*, Kolkata: Oriental Book Company, 1998, p. xv.
53. Das, op. cit., p. 171.
54. Bhattacharjee, 1989, op. cit, p. 40.
55. Ibid.
56. Quoted in S.C. Biswas, *Bhulibe Ki Praanaantey?*, Silchar: no publisher, 1998, pp. 81-2.
57. '*Aro dukkho Assam-er Sylheti Swarashtra Mantri Basanta Kumar Das porjonto gaa korlen na*'; see Amitava Chaudhuri, 'Nirbashita Tumi', in S. Debray (ed.), *Sribhumi Srihatta: Sreehatter Samskriti Bishayak Prabandha Samkalan*, Durgapur Srihatta Sammilani, p. 1. (Translation from Bengali mine.)
58. Abdul Matlib Majumdar, 'Lokopriya Gopinath Bordoloi: A Devotee of Mahatma Gandhi', in Lily Mazumder Baruah (ed.), *Lokopriya Gopinath Bordoloi: An Architect of Modern India*, New Delhi: Gyan Publishing House, 1992, p. 247.
59. Bidyut Chakrabarty, 'The "hut" and the "axe": The 1947 Sylhet Referendum', *The Indian Economic and Social History Review,* 39(4), 2002, p. 343.
60. Makhan Lal Kar, *Muslims in Assam Politics*, New Delhi: Vikas Publishing House, 1997, p. 49.
61. Ibid.
62. *Amrita Bazar Patrika*, 6 July 1947.
63. Kar, op. cit., p. 49.
64. Bijan Bihari Purakayastha, *Swadhinata Sangrame Srihatta*, op. cit. (Translation from Bengali mine.)
65. Chakrabarty, op. cit., p. 349.

CHAPTER THREE

Being Sylheti in Assam (1874-1947)

What did it mean to be a Sylheti in colonial Assam? Historically and culturally a part of Bengal, Sylhet along with the neighbouring Cachar, were incorpo-rated into the Chief Commissionership of Assam in 1874. Here they stayed in an uneasy partnership until the Referendum and Partition took place in 1947. Together, the areas formed the two valleys of Assam, which was now elevated to the status of a full province. According to the official correspondence of the East India Company (which annexed Assam in 1826 following the signing of Treaty of Yandaboo with the occupying Burmese state), the move was for administrative convenience and economic benefit, as Assam alone did not produce enough revenue to sustain itself unless supported by its thickly populated Sylheti-speaking neighbourhood. Some other reasons forwarded by the British administration included that Cachar was as backward as Assam, that the lush forests of Cachar required constant supervision, and that it would not be 'wise to split the tea districts' of Assam, Cachar and Sylhet.[1] Either way, the move was unexpected for a number of reasons, particularly because Sylhet had historically, culturally and economically been a part of Bengal, and neither the Sylhetis nor the Assamese supported the move. Both, in fact, demanded that the unification be revoked and that Sylhet go back to Bengal where it rightfully belonged.

The transfers, especially of Sylhet, were crucial for Assam as a whole for several reasons. First, the population of Sylhet alone matched that of the whole of Assam which would go on to heighten the Sylheti-Assamese discord with an increased sense of competition; second, the Sylheti population was predominantly Bengali-speaking; and third, in the overall context of the newly-expanded province, Muslims (a majority of them from Sylhet) now constituted almost a third of the population.[2] Until 1874, the Brahmaputra Valley, or what now came to be known as 'Assam proper', had consisted of only the five modern-day Assamese-speaking Hindu majority districts of Darrang, Kamrup, Lakhimpur, Nowgong and Sibasagar. These represented the Ahom kingdom established in the thirteenth century, which more or less came to an end with the British extension in 1826. On the other hand, the newly attached Surma Valley, consisting of the Bengali-speaking districts of Sylhet and Cachar possessed a large Muslim population. There were almost no Assamese-speaking elements in the Surma Valley, and a majority of the population in Goalpara the westernmost district of Assam spoke Bengali. The Brahmaputra and Surma valleys were now divided by the hills districts (of the Khasi and Jaintia Hills) into two separate linguistic and cultural zones, one of which was primarily Hindu and Assamese-speaking and the other overwhelmingly Muslim and Bengali-speaking. The term *Assam*, which had originally stood for the erstwhile Ahom territory alone and later for the whole Brahmaputra Valley, was now given a wider significance to denote the newly emerged linguistically plural province.[3]

The people‘s reaction to this transfer, writes a local historian, was 'quick and profound'.[4] Most Sylhetis and the Assamese condemned the decision even before it was actually implemented. At least three separate memoranda were submitted by the people of the Surma Valley urging the British administration to revise its decision. The first, addressed to the lieutenant-governor of Bengal, was submitted by the Sylhet People's Association and was signed by 2,000 Sylhetis who pointed to the longstanding cultural similarities that Sylhet shared with the rest of Bengal. It also expressed the fear that the transfer would force the people to lose out on the valuable acts and regulations of the Bengal Council, the Lieutenant Governor of Bengal, the Bengal Board of Revenue and the Calcutta High Court, which would not only result in deterioration in the standard of administration but also in the social and cultural degradation of the people.[5] The petitioners further pointed out that the transfer would snap all existing connections that Sylhet had with Calcutta leading to a cultural gap; they even objected to be called as Assamese.[6]

Soon afterwards, another memorandum was submitted by the people of Sylhet, and a third by the inhabitants of Cachar. Among other things, these communications again pointed out the rich cultural heritage that Sylhet shared with Bengal, the lack of communication systems between Bengal and Assam, and the anxiety that the transfer would result in deterioration in the standard of administration and the overall cultural degradation of Sylhet.[7]

The first generation of vocal and fire-brand Sylhetis (such as Kamini Kumar Chanda, Brajendra Narayan Choudhury and Khirode Chandra Deb) voiced the demand for a restoration to Bengal on linguistic grounds. Other high-profile leaders—Basanta Kumar Das (later home minister of Assam), Rai Bahadur Nagendra Nath Chowdhury and *zamindars* (landowners) such as Khan Bahadur Muhammed Bakht Mazumdar, Khan Bahadur Syed Abdul Majid, Khan Bahadur Allauddin Ahmed Chowdhury, etc.—also supported the movement to reunite Sylhet with Bengal, and raised the issue in almost all important political forums. The Assamese, too, in a rare instance of unanimity with theSylhetis, endorsed the demand for transfer. At this time, both the Muslims and Hindus of Sylhet were united in their opposition to the transfer. With the onset of communal politics in the 1940s, however, the stance of Assam's (and Sylhet's) Muslim political leaders would slowly change to support Sylhet's separation from the rest of Assam and its amalgamation to the newly formed state of (East) Pakistan. In fact, as early as 1926, the Brahmaputra Valley Muslim leader Sir Syed Saadullah Khan would argue that as long as Sylhet remained with Assam, Muslims who constituted one-third of the province's population would remain a 'respectable minority and hold the balance of Assam's electoral politics.'[8]

This would have serious repercussions in the years to come, however, especially with the steady growth of communalism and resultant demands for a partition of the country on the basis of religion. With the establishment of the Muslim League and two separate stints of Muslim League ministries in Assam, in the 1930s and 1940s, the issue of Sylhet would take a communal twist, when the Muslim community would begin to articulate demands for the absorption of the entire province of Assam into Jinnah's proposal of a six-province Pakistan. But for the moment, a Sylhet Reunion Movement was started by prominent Sylheti leaders, though its history was replete with distrust, jealousy and rivalry, and led to a wedge between both the two valleys and the two religious communities, the Hindus and Muslims.[9] Soon, the Assamese too became somewhat hesitant to pursue the issue of Sylhet's retransfer out of fear that such a move could affect Assam's status as a separate province, and that other districts (such as Goalpara and Cachar, both Bengali-speaking) might also demand amalgamation with Bengal, which would drastically reduce the size and political status of Assam as a province. Though, of course, the press and politicians strove to make it abundantly clear that, in general, the Assamese public opinion stood firmly behind the separation of Sylhet from the rest of Assam.

The failure of the Sylhet Reunion Movement led to a sense of growing sense of loss within the Sylheti community at large. But although the issue lost its fire after the initial spark, it never did completely die out.[10] The Sylhetis were somewhat pacified when 14 other Bengal districts were attached to Assam between 1905 and 1912, following the Partition of Bengal. And yet, in 1912, these new borders were revoked and all other Bengali provinces returned to Bengal—except Sylhet. Once again, Assam's two valleys went back to being a Chief Commissioner's province in 1912. It is this 'shunting like a train-wagon', once to the east and then to the west, that produced a unique Sylheti identity, writes Krishna Kumar Palchoudhury.[11] The uncertainty that was generated by this back and forth led to a sense of 'unity of common fate'[12] among the people of Sylhet, '… Hindus and Muslims alike'.[13]

Soon, however, Sylhet and its neighbouring areas emerged as important colonial towns, known mostly for the vast expanses of tea gardens located on top of hillocks or *tillas*. In one of his short stories, a Sylheti author named Bibhash De offers a description of one such colonial town in Sylhet district:

In the mid 1940s, the town of Srimangal in Sylhet District was an important business center for many nearby tea plantations, or tea gardens as they were more commonly called. A few of these were owned by Englishmen. These owners actually lived in the plantations, and made their home in this far, forgotten corner of India. When they longed for a taste of Home [sic], they came to the general store in town, called the South Sylhet Supply Stores. It was well-stocked with all types of things—from Huntley & Palmers Biscuits and Black Magic Chocolates to butter that could be bought in blocks out of the refrigerator. Rows of jars of Keiller's Dundee Marmalades and tins of Capstan cigarettes gave the place a distinct aura of the British Isles. The Sahebs and the Memsahebs got into their Jeeps or Morris Minors or Staff Cars, came to the store, and loaded up on supplies. They lingered and chitchatted with the Indian owner and caught up with what all was going on in the town, and with the Big War. The owner had all kinds of strange stories to tell. One story, for example, had that some disembodied being often visited his store at night. Although the doors were locked and windows were shut, he often found in the morning fresh pieces of water hyacinth on the floor. The Englishmen listened to his stories with great attention, and then laughed all the way home.[14]

The social distance between the colonial officers and the Sylheti babus, professionals and traders was often less than that with the local Assamese. The British saw this group of English-educated *bhadralok* from Bengal as a 'buffer' or intervening layer against the local Assamese population, while the locals often considered them as collaborators of the British and encountered them as the everyday face of colonialism. In turn, the English-educated Sylhetis possessed a certain air of sophistication and maintained a studied distance from the locals, often patronised them socially, at the same time blocked their entries into government services whenever possible, when the first English-educated Assamese began applying for those positions.

THE *BHADRALOK*: THE SYLHETI MIDDLE CLASS IN ASSAM

Against this backdrop, no discussion on 'Sylheti-ness' can put aside the issue of class, or what it meant to be a *bhadralok* in the newly formed Assam province. In the district headquarters of the colonial government of Assam, the Sylheti *bhadralok* were the quintessential *babus*, or government employees in clerical positions, disproportionately employed in the provincial government offices. They were also omnipresent in the emerging professions of law, teaching and even in trading and contract jobs. Since the early 19th century, the Sylhetis became a largely mobile population in colonial Assam, regularly moving out of their hometowns in significant numbers to other parts of the newly constituted province, including the Brahmaputra Valley in search of jobs. With a head start in English education, many of them (including my grandfather) secured government jobs with relative ease, built new homes in the Brahmaputra Valley or Shillong while regularly returned to their ancestral homes in Sylhet on special occasions only. As early as 1901, the *Census of India* recorded that 'Sylhetis who are good clerks and are enterprising traders are found, in small numbers, in most of the districts of the [Assam] province.'[15]

The provincial administration was not prepared to build up appropriate educational infrastructure for the simple reason that it could recruit Bengal's surplus educated personnel to fill the offices at a minimum cost.[16] Strictly speaking, of course, there was no obvious reason for the British administration not to appoint Sylhetis in administrative positions, as Sylhet was now officially a part of Assam. And, according to Sylheti interviewees, because many Sylhetis had reached high positions within the bureaucracy, they were often able to block the appointment of the few Assamese applicants for such jobs with relative ease. Having said so, however, it is important to note that an English-educated Assamese middle class was still nascent as that time, and that its prominent members were more involved in the restoration of the Assamese language to its former status as the official language of the province which the British had changed to Bengali in the entire period 1834-74 for administrative convenience.

When the province was re-constituted into a Chief Commissionership in 1912 (following the revocation of the Partition of Bengal) the number of literate persons in Sylhet alone was some 132,500, against only 144,600 in the whole of the Brahmaputra Valley. In 1935, the number of recognised schools in Cachar and Sylhet (under Calcutta University) alone was almost equal to the total number of schools in the rest of the province.[17] Out of 1,346 students who matriculated from Assam's schools between 1882 and 1899, 335 (25 per cent) were natives of the Brahmaputra Valley, 629 (47 per cent) of the Surma Valley and 382 (28 per cent) of other provinces.[18]

With Assam government posts not yet clearly earmarked with regards to 'valley of origin', Sylhet thus obtained the lion's share of jobs under the government.[19]

In 1874, Shillong became the capital of the new province, and droves of job-seekers inevitably flocked to the new power centre. 'All these [Sylheti] clerks, teachers, lawyers and petty businessmen dominated the show for a long time giving an air of self-estimation,' writes Tanmay Bhattacharjee in his book, *The Sylhet Referendum*. 'At least in the corridors of the administration in the capital, Assamese language was not heard so much.'[20] Given Shillong's large concentration of government departments, particularly those of the Accountant-general of Assam, multiple Sylheti settlements soon sprouted throughout the town, especially in the popular neighbourhoods like Laban, Rilbong and Jail Road. My grandfather too purchased a house in 1942 in the heart of Laban, near the Bengali-medium Laban Girls School. Bhattacharjee writes that though some Assamese had started a cultural meeting ground called the Assam Club in Shillong, 'way back in the late nineteenth century the Bengali presence in Shillong was far more conspicuous.'[21] The Sylheti relationship with Shillong remained strong even after Partition. During the subsequent decades, a large number of displaced Sylhetis ended up migrating to this picturesque hilly town, where relatives and friends were plentiful and where jobs in the Assamese government offices were still to be had. This dynamic continued at least until the transfer of the state capital to Gauhati (later Guwahati) in 1972 along with the entire infrastucture of the Accountant-General's office where large number of Sylhetis were employed.

This historical and sentimental connection of Sylhetis with Shillong can be discerned in the works of the well-known novelist Amit Chaudhuri, whose mother moved from Sylhet to Shillong (and eventually to Calcutta) after the Sylhet Referendum in 1947. The images of both Sylhet and Shillong appear, even if fleetingly, in almost all of his novels. For instance, in *A Strange and Sublime Address*, the character Shonamama recalls his own childhood in

Sylhet 'when India was one big piece and the British ruled us,' followed by a move to Shillong with its 'mountains and waterfalls'.[22] In *Freedom Song*, too, Mini remembers her childhood in Puran Lane in Sylhet during the pre-Partition days. 'The votes were counted after the referendum,' writes Chaudhuri, 'their country was gone … after two months they packed their things and took a train to Gauhati and then a bus to Shillong.'[23] Again, in an evocative article titled 'At the Edge of the Cloud', Chaudhuri writes that Shillong was the town to which 'my mother and her family moved, just before Sylhet, first part of Bengal, then Assam, was lost to Pakistan with the referendum.' The memory of loss and relocation, both territorial and emotional, thus linger in his writings more than six decades after the Sylhet Referendum and Partition.

Amitava Chaudhuri, a well-known Sylheti writer, admits that though Sylhet was a part of Assam,

> we were Assamese only in name. We had no connection with Gauhati. All connections and contacts were with Calcutta. Far from knowing the Assamese language—though I was a Sylheti—the first time I saw an Assamese was when I completed matriculation and came to Shantiniketan.[24]

For the Sylheti frequent traveller, the journey from Sylhet to Shillong was often an arduous one, both mentally and physically, as my grandmother would often recall. Tanmay Bhattacharjee, a Cachar-based academic, recaptures the journey in the following words:

> Some part of the journey was made by boat, some part on foot and the steep hills had to be negotiated on the back of the sturdy human carriers, the coolies, and the journey in the nineteenth century was most exciting and strenuous, and a few had the opportunity to have such an experience but in the twentieth century the situation changed for the better.Many ladies too, reached Shillong along with their consorts experiencing such travel hardships.[25]

Silchar, the headquarters of Cachar, was established the same year as Sylhet, mainly to serve the tea gardens that dotted the Surma Valley. Over the years, the Sylheti *bhadralok* also settled in the various district headquarters of the Brahmaputra Valley; many established communities on the plains of Gauhati, Assam's most populous district, which boasted of excellent education facilities, and rail- and river-based communications. However, many others moved into the tea districts of Upper Assam, where they took up positions as clerks or petty tradesmen in support of the plantations. Gradually, the Sylheti *babus* became a distinctly visible group in the urban areas of Assam, their homes usually located on the more expensive lands on the banks of the Brahmaputra close to the Deputy Commissioner's courts.

The noted Assamese intellectual Gunaviram Baruah wrote a long article in 1885 to discuss Bengali-Assamese relations, which were already tending to develop into a love-and-hate spectrum, says historian Amalendu Guha. He [Gunaviram Baruah] noted that, whether desirable or not, the Bengali *babu* or *bhadralok* had become the model for the growing Assamese middle class.[26] Bengali-medium schools opened everywhere and the Sylheti *bhadralok* were happy for the status and power they had in relation to the locals—who, in turn, soon began to view them with respect intermingled with fear and, over time, impatience.

Many of the urban Sylhetis in Assam like my grandfather would continue to return to Sylhet annually, but increasingly only on special occasions such as marriages and festivals. Elsewhere I have discussed the notions of the *desher baari* (village home) and *town-er baari* (town home)[126] within the Sylheti discourse —in which, with increased job opportunities and migration to cities, the village-based joint families of the past gradually started to give way to city-based nuclear families, even as the latter became infused with urbanity with more and more boys leaving for employment to cities such as Shillong, Guwahati, etc., and returning periodically to the hometown. The distance between Shillong and Sylhet was 86 miles, out of which 40 miles were across hilly areas. 'We had to stop several times at different gates as much of the road was open for only one-way traffic,' recalled my father travelling between the two towns just before Independence.

> Part of the road after the Lailongkot gate was steep. There were no trees and it was really scary to look down … also for 16-18 miles we could not see clearly due to the thick fog. After we crossed the second gate at Pynursla, we could begin to see some of the water bodies in Sylhet from the tall mountain tops. Then we drove all the way down to Dawki and from there it was a straight drive to Sylhet.

Surama Ghatak, in her autobiography *Surma Nadir Deshe* (In the land of the River Surma), also describes her childhood journeys from Shillong to Sylhet during the annual festival of Durga Puja. 'As soon as the puja vacations began, we left for the [Sylhet] plains,' she wrote. 'For us it was a new country . . . this beautiful country has green paddy fields, lakes, rivers and the autumn blue skies.'[28] She then describes her journey to Sylhet town, from where her family would proceed to the village home:

We had to travel about 30 miles by train to reach Kulaura Station. The train would be crowded with people returning home [to Sylhet] for the pujas, so much discussions, so many different views from the train window . . . my mother and aunts made all the puja arrangements, such a lot of food was cooked, there were prayers in the evenings. In every home in the neighbourhood relatives visited, every house had the air of festivity . . . the puja days used to pass like a dream . . . I can never forget my desher bari. When the pujas and all the fun ended, we returned from the [Sylhet] plains to the [Shillong] hills.[29]

Among Sylhetis, I realised that there usually exists a sense of being culturally and linguistically somewhat ' different' from all other Bengalis. They take pride in this exclusiveness, and particularly extol the Sylheti qualities, in particular the capacity to laugh at themselves.[30]

Older Sylhetis often shared with me quintessential Sylheti sayings such as, 'There are only two countries in the world, Sylhet and Bilet [*Vilayet* or England]' or that '*Sylhet-e modhyomo nasti*' (There is no mediocrity in Sylhet). Some Sylhetis also took pride in telling me that Sylhet's rich history is borne out by the facts that even the Chinese pilgrim Hieuen Tsang, who travelled to the Subcontinent in around 630 AD, had made references to the area in his well-known account of his journey, saying that Sylhet was the land of great philosophers and holy men such as Mahaprabhu Chaitanya and Shah Jalal. In a similar vein, Amitava Chaudhuri writes that this Sylheti pride was based on the following factors: 'Hindu-Muslim unity, high rate of education, women's progress, comparatively less poverty, competitiveness, many great leaders of India have been Sylhetis and the fact that Sylhet was the only Bengal district which Rabindranath Tagore had composed a poem about.'[31]

Yet it can also be argued that the sense of being a Sylheti was sharpened after the district's unexpected inclusion into Assam, a comparatively less-developed province of the British Raj, where the benefits of English education and liberalism were yet to percolate. Such a situation subsequently provided the Sylhetis with an opportunity to dominate the lower and middle bureaucracy, and in effect to project themselves as representatives of the British in this distant part of the Raj. As such, the economically and socially powerful Sylhetis frequently displayed cultural superiority over the natives. This attitude became more pronounced as the emergent Assamese middle class struggled to announce its arrival, demanding a share of the government jobs and finding itself a minority in the urban middle-class milieu. Of particular significance was that, in 1901, close to half of the population of Assam spoke Bengali. In 1926, Dewan Wasil Chowdhury (a representative to the Assam Council from Sylhet) stated in the Council that the ' bars, benches and subordinate services' which were once dominated by the Bengalis[from Calcutta] were at present manned by the 'Sylhetis'.[32]

To the Assamese Hindus in particular, who were the real competitors for government jobs, the complex went as deep as to gradually make them intolerant of things non-indigenous. They also became increasingly sensitive to their 'otherness' from the Bengalis—or Sylhetis, to be precise. What made matters more delicate was that the colonial masters imposed the Bengali language upon the province for the entire period from 1834 to 1874. As soon as this was changed in favour of Assamese, Sylhet was quickly thrust upon the incipient province, thus replacing only the form of what the Assamese saw as the overall 'Bengali' dominance. In this way, Assamese nationalism, which developed in opposition to the Sylheti identity, acquired an anti-Bengali and later overall anti-'outsider' character. The conceptual and organizational roots of Assamese nationalism began to take shape after the mid-20th century through political mobilization by the Assamese middle classes on the language issue, which gradually transformed into a constructed notion of identity in Assam. However, even if the Assamese were able to deal with the issue of the Sylheti Hindu domination in the services and social sector, the crunch came with the beginning of a new flow of migrants also from East Bengal, but different districts. This was the migration into Assam of the Muslim underclass from the Bengali-speaking districts of East Bengal—Mymensingh, Bogura, Pabna and Rangpur—who brought another demographic influx into the Brahmaputra Valley as agricultural labour. What was essentially more of a middle-class Assamese-Sylheti rivalry over jobs and representation in local elected bodies, slowly began to transform into one of the most complicated issues in Assam's politics over the subsequent years.

NOTES

1. Jayanta Bhushan Bhattacharjee, *Reaction of the People of Surma Valley to transfer of the Valley to Assam*, 1874,

Proceedings of the North East India History Association, Tenth Session, Shillong.

2. Amalendu Guha, *Planter Raj to Swaraj: Freedom Struggle and Electoral Politics in Assam, 1826-1947*, New Delhi: ICHR, 1977, p. 23.
3. This paragraph is largely based on Amalendu Guha, *Planter Raj to Swaraj: Freedom Struggle and Electoral Politics in Assam, 1885-1947*, Calcutta: Peoples Publishing House, 1977, p. 25.
4. Ajit K. Neogy quoted in Bhattacharjee, op. cit., p. 448.
5. Bhattacharjee, op. cit., p. 449.
6. Ibid, p. 449.
7. Amita Roy, 'The Reunion Movement in Surma Valley (Assam), 1917-1928', unpublished M.Phil dissertation, North-Eastern Hill University, Shillong, pp. 11-12.
8. Guha, 1977, op. cit., p. 135.
9. Makhan Lal Kar, *Muslims in Assam Politics*, New Delhi: Vikas Publishing House, 1990, p. 112.
10. Sanghamitra Paul Choudhury, 'Sylhet Referendum-1947', unpublished M.Phil dissertation, North-Eastern Hill University, Shillong, 1992, p. 10.
11. Krishna Kumar Palchoudhury, 'Sylhet, Sylhetitwa O' Sylhet-er Ahonkar', in S. Debray (ed.), *Sribhumi Srihatta: Sreehatter Samskriti Bishayak Prabandha Samkalan,* Durgapur Srihatta Sammilani, p. 1. (Translation from Bengali mine.)
12. Ibid., p. 1. Translation from Bengali mine.
13. Ibid.
14. http://www.geocities.com/bibhasde/stories.html accessed on 16/7/2007.
15. *Census of India*, Government of India, 1901.

16. Guha, op. cit., p. 47.
17. Tanmay Bhattacharjee, *The Sylhet Referendum: A Study in Retrospect*, Silchar, 2006, p. 34.
18. Guha, 1997, op. cit., p. 47.
19. Ibid.
20. Bhattacharjee, 2006, op. cit., p. 33.
21. Ibid., p. 33.
22. Amit Chaudhuri, *Three Novels*, London: Picador, 2001, p. 53.
23. Chaudhuri, ibid., p. 380.
24. Amitava Chaudhuri, in Debray (ed.), *Sribhumi Srihatta: Sreehatter Samskriti Bishayak Prabandha Samkalan*, Durgapur Srihatta Sammilani.
25. Bhattacharjee, 2006, op. cit., p. 35.
26. Guha. op. cit.. p. 55
27. Anindita Dasgupta, 2001, 'Denial and Resistance: Sylhet Partition "Refugees" in Assam', *Contemporary South Asia*, 10: 3 (1 November 2001), pp. 58-83.
28. Surama Ghatak, *Surma Nadir Deshe*, Anushtup, Kolkata 2001, p. 4. (Translation from Bengali mine.)
29. Ibid., p. 4
30. Cracking 'Sylheti' jokes (or digs at Sylhetis themselves) are a common feature in Sylheti social gatherings. I have personally experienced such gatherings in the years that I lived in Assam.
31. A. Chaudhuri, 'Nirbashita Tumi', in S. Debray (ed.), *Sribhumi Srihatta*, p. 158. (Translation from Bengali mine.)
32. Cited in Arun Bhuyan et al., *Political History of Assam*, vol. 2, *1920-1939*, Guwahati: Government of Assam, 1978, p. 292.

CHAPTER FOUR

East Bengal Muslim Migration into Assam

Since the last decade of the nineteenth century, landless Muslim peasants from the East Bengal districts of Mymensingh, Noakhali, Pabna and Bogura began to migrate to the neighbouring province of Assam with the blessings of the colonial masters in search of agricultural land. In Assam, they were loosely known as *Mymensinghias* (as most of them migrated from the Mymensingh district of East Bengal) and, in later years, simply as *Miyas*. At this time, these landless peasants were proletariats in a real sense: they had nothing to sell but their labour, and soon they were employed in large numbers as agricultural labourers on the sprawling lands of Assam, particularly in the Brahmaputra Valley. Following this steady migration, the countryside of Assam began to see the spread and consolidation of cultivated land as opposed to the wasteland and forests of previous years. Such wilderness, of course, varied according to climate and soil but on the whole included marshes, *beels* (small waterbodies) and woodlands offering many resources, grasslands, coastal foreshores and *chars* (the sandbars along the middle and lower course of the river Brahmaputra) often haunted by wild animals. Many migrants built new homes on the banks and the *chars* which the native Assamese supposedly did not care to use. Small groups of such landless people, coming at different times from different parts of East Bengal, soon filled up the riverine countryside of Assam, struggling against floods, rains, epidemics and erosion, and devoted themselves to clearing and sowing the land. Some even grew prosperous by reclaiming land.

For reasons rooted in the history of the region, the Brahmaputra Valley had an abundance of cultivable land when the British occupied it in 1826. Indeed, at the turn of the century the greatest obstacle to the extension of agriculture in Assam had been the absence of a labouring class. While in the Surma Valley and the districts of Kamrup and Goalpara, agricultural labourers were extremely scarce, in Central and Upper Assam they were practically non-existent; as such, initially the Assamese landlords were happy to find a cheap and steady labour supply for their sprawling fields.

But on the flip-side, the number of Bengali-speakers in Assam continued to be replenished by these Muslim peasants from East Bengal, who crowded into the agricultural fields, providing cheap labour for the landowners and purchased land wherever possible.Clusters of new little thatched huts soon began to appear on the banks of the Brahmaputra and with them began the complaints, threats and pleas from the established Assamese villages. This happened in the early twentieth century, especially in Nagaon district in central Assam, where the migrants had lodged on the edges of the river or on unfarmed, abandoned land that belonged to the natives.

In the pre-colonial years, Assam had developed a remarkable capacity to hold together disparate (sometimes mutually hostile, at other times innovative) cultures in a functional partnership under the umbrella of an 'Assamese' identity, which was both fluid and inclusive. The colonial years saw a change in attitude first due to the very large flow of migrants compared to the trickle of earlier times. Second, with the disruption of the traditional economy, avenues for income became limited and competition over scarce resources was not entirely unnatural. Third and finally, British divide-and-rule policy played a significant role in changing this liberal attitude, and the principal instrument through which the British achieved this end in Assam was the colonial census.

The first colonial census of Assam was carried out in 1872. Officially aimed at providing accurate information about the province, in effect the explicit data on place of birth, religion and language highlighted the society's differences and deeply influenced its communal politics. The colonial census not only created types and classes of people but also labelled and drew boundaries around identities, thus transforming indigenous ideas of differences into a politics of community. In the already tense situation following Assam's amalgamation with Sylhet in 1874, it was not very difficult to ignite scepticism in the Brahmaputra Valley over the more recent issue of peasant migration from East Bengal, the peasants who not only spoke various dialects of Bengali but also professed a different faith, Islam. Not unsurprisingly then, the Assamese society began to chaff under the demographic transformation.

This new peasant migration began as early as

1891, at a time when Assam was just beginning to accept the fait accompli of the amalgamation of Sylhet and Cachar, though at that time the flow was not substantial. Initially a majority of peasants came from Rangpur, but thereafter each successive census recorded a majority from Mymensingh district instead. The well-known Assamese writer Syed Abdul Malik provides a vivid description of such migration in his much-acclaimed Assamese-language novel *Rupaborir Polosh*:

> carrying two hand-woven *lungis*, a white cotton cap, a *banian* or a shirt, a dagger, one or two aluminium vessels and pots on their shoulders, they left their familiar villages, familiar land and began their journey towards Assam...some walked miles after miles to reach the railway station, some spent nights under the tall trees and ate the puffed rice they carried from home. They sold their ducks, chicken and goats to buy a third class train-ticket and wherever possible, bribed the guard or the ticket-checker with a little money to be able to travel without a ticket ... and along the way wherever they were found out, they jumped off the train.[1]

Writing in 1891, however, Sir Edward Gait, the Census Commissioner, seemed to have little premonition of the implications of this migration:

> A certain number of persons from the neighbouring Bengal districts of Mymensingha, Dacca and Rongpur have crossed

the boundary and settled down in Sylhet and Goalpara, but they can scarcely be called immigration. *They have moved only a few miles from their original homes, and the accident of boundary alone has brought them within the limits of Assam.*[2] [Emphasis mine]

The census of 1901, in turn, reported only a trickle of East Bengal peasant migration into Assam. Before 1911, however, a significant change was observed, as peasants from Mymensingh began to migrate to Assam in large numbers, apparently driven by the pressure on soil at home. The Census Report of 1911 was the first to comment on the increasing movement of settlers to the *char* areas of Goalpara from districts in Bengal, registering a rush for land along the Brahmaputra to the northeast and in Hill Tippera to the southeast. This cheap and fertile land attracted a growing number of cultivators from the lower reaches in the densely populated East Bengal districts of Bogra, Pabna, Mymensingh and Dacca, where the riparian areas suffered from the washing away of soil. The East Bengal migrant settlements were more common along the Brahmaputra, but in many instances they also penetrated far inland; parties in search of land had even been found near the Bhutan border. The population of Goalpara on the western border of Assam with Bengal, which had increased only by 1.4 per cent in 1881-91 and 2 per cent in 1891-1901, now shot up by 30 per cent between 1901 and 1911.[3] It must be pointed out, however, that the population increase in 1911 also coincided with the creation of the province of East Bengal and Assam after the Partition of Bengal in 1905 (subsequently revoked in 1911). Therefore, the increase could be partially explained due to this factor, among others.

As discussed, the colonial census provided a cultural map of the province, bringing numbers into the realm of everyday life and driving a wedge between communities. It also set off contradictions and conflict in the already uneasy relationship between the natives and migrants, as the census proposed a migrant who could now be defined in both time and space—one who could now be counted and whose age, sex, occupation, religion, place of birth and language could be easily classified. The decade of 1911-21 showed an unexpectedly large increase in the number of peasant-migrants in the Brahmaputra Valley. In 1916, the Director of Land Records put forward a proposal for a 'special colonising officer' who would assist the settlement of incoming migrants and coordinate the work of all districts into which migration was taking place. Although this proposal was supported by many District Commissioners, it did not appeal to the then-Commissioner of Assam, and was not raised again until Sir William Reid, the well-known executive councillor of Nowgong district, addressed the government in 1920 with a similar suggestion.

The Census Report of 1921 described the East Bengal migrants as 'merely the advance guards of a huge army following close at their heels',[4] and indeed, the sex and age figures given in provincial tables from that year showed that colonists were settling not only as individuals but as families. Between 1911 and 1921, the total number of villages in Assam increased by 3,000 (to 32,275)—the growth most marked in Goalpara, Darrang and Nowgong, where there were large numbers of migrants from East Bengal, about 85 per cent of whom were Muslim and 15 per cent were Hindu.[5] The East Bengal settlers increased more than 'fourfold' in this decade in the Brahmaputra Valley.[6] The census also registered some 6,000 people from Mymensingh and Rangpur who had settled in the distant Garo Hills straddling the two valleys, though Sibsagar and Lakhimpur in northern Assam were yet to feel the pressure of the migrants. Some 20 per cent of Goalpara's population was now of migrant origin. The population density in the district had increased from 152 to 193 by 1921—and was highest in Mancachar *thana* (police-station jurisdiction) at 567.

Thus, a migrant population that had not been only a trickle in 1901 in spite of official patronage had become, within just a few years, one to seriously reckon with. With this steady flow, the stirrings of discontent over control of land began to appear slowly. The protests of the local Assamese against such free migration persisted through the 1920s and early 1930s. If the migration continued at this rate, it was now feared, the Assamese would soon be turned into a linguistic minority in their own traditional homeland. So, some sections of Assamese society raised the slogan of the 'Assamese race' being in danger; in 1926, the prominent Assamese leader Ambikagiri Roy Choudhury floated the protectionist Asom Surakshini Sabha to propagate the Assamese cause, joined also by Nilamoni Phukan, another Assamese stalwart. It was then that the demand for the containment of further influx of East Bengal Muslim immigrants into Goalpara and the rest of the Brahmaputra Valley began to be increasingly raised as a political issue.[7]

In reality though, some ad hoc restrictive measures on indiscriminate migrant settlement appeared to already be in place. The *Report of the Line System Committee*, a valuable document on East Bengal peasant migration, notes that from a letter of the deputy commissioner of Kamrup, it seems that the system of drawing a line across which new migrants should not be permitted to settle had already begun in the Barpeta sub-division; and, according to a similar letter from the Deputy Commissioner of Nowgong, lines had also been laid down in villages to restrict indiscriminate settlements by the migrants. It should be noted, however, that such decisions originated entirely with the district officers concerned, and was not adopted in execution of any government order. That said, the government did not interfere with the new system—eventually referred to as the Line System—which gradually developed in slightly different forms in various districts of Assam.

THE LINE SYSTEM OF 1920

The term 'Line System' refers to all restrictions and control regarding land settlements on all non-natives in Assam. Initiated in 1920, it first came into operation in Nowgong before being extended to all other districts that were also experiencing large influx of migrants—though it was never extended to the entirety of Assam. Where the number of new migrant settlers in a village was small, no reservation of land was deemed necessary; nor did the Line System come into operation in the permanently settled areas (Goalpara and Sylhet), despite the fact that most early migrants settled in Goalpara. The purpose of the Line System was put forth clearly by the Nowgong Superintendent of Police, K.R. Chowdhury: 'The Line System was introduced [ostensibly] with a view to keep peace and order between the indigenous people and the immigrants and to protect the natural rights and interests of the local people till their assimilation.'[8]

On 19 June 1923, when the colonizing officer raised the issue of some native Assamese willingly subletting their land to migrants, the government ordered that if such lands were covered by annual *pattas* (leases), these transfers would be immediately revoked. As such, a full classification of villages was made, and lines were printed on maps separating the lands of the nativesfrom those open to settlement by the migrants. On the question of granting *pattas*, the government was clear: If converted into periodic *pattas*, the lands would have quickly passed into the hands of the migrants and the whole Line System would have become ineffective. In order to avoid this from happening, the native Assamese were given special, non-transferable annual *pattas* while the migrants were allowed to possess periodic pattas on their side of the line.

At this time, S.N. Mackenzie, the Commissioner of the Assam Valley Division, undertook a critical action: for the first time he officially defined the word *immigrant*. This word, he ordered, would subsequently include persons from all districts of Bengal and the Surma Valley, but would not include tea-garden coolies or former coolies. 'This meaning will also be attached to the word Mymensingia wherever it appears in official papers,' the order stated.[9] In his standing order, it was clearly stipulated that the term *Mymensinghia* would henceforth be dropped and the word *immigrant* substituted in all official papers. It further stated that 'immigrants' could not acquire the same rights as the Assamese *ryots* (peasants). This, at any rate, was what had been officially clarified; but the reality was often quite different.

The operations of the Line System clearly demonstrated the half-heartedness that went into its making. The Line was an irritant to the migrants while it also did not satisfy the natives. The new restrictions did achieve one thing, however, the lines sharply outlined the differences between the two communities: the natives and the migrants. Clashes between the two communities now became more frequent and sometimes, even turned violent. On the other hand, the British managed to retain their own control over local resources by overseeing the allotment and disbursement of landholdings, designing 'enclaves' of communities, changing cropping patterns (because the natives and migrants had different priorities and expertise in agriculture), and dividing Assam's population into two opposing units, by controlling and regulating their access to the province's limited resources.

The restrictions on settlements, or the Line System, were initially applied only to *Mymensinghias*. But migrants from other districts of Bengal, especially Dacca, Noakhali and the Surma Valley, soon started arriving, and by a government order of 22 August 1924, the term *immigrant* was extended to describe all East Bengal migrants regardless of their district of origin. The Surma Valley migrants also started settling down in present-day Hojai and Namati *mauzas*, where a vast tract of land was set apart for them known as the 'Sylheti Block', where they were allowed to settle without any restriction.[10] The same order also stipulated that settlements by other communities like the Sikhs, Keyas (or Marwaris) and up-country traders would also require government sanction, though no restrictions seem to have been put on them or on former tea-garden-labour most of whom had been hired from in and around the state of Bihar. However, they were also later classified as 'immigrants', and brought under the Line System. A decade later, the Keyas were also declared as 'immigrants' by a government order of 3 December 1935, as they had in some cases purchased land from the Assamese and sold these to the East Bengal migrants. Finally, apart from the lines between the Assamese and the various migrants, there were also 'lines' between the migrants themselves. In these cases, there were no restrictions on transfer and subletting as in the case of the Assamese lines, since, wrote Deputy Commissioner Mackenzie, 'these immigrants are all able to protect themselves against one another.'[11]

Overall, historian Amalendu Guha is categorical

about the ineffectiveness of the Line System as a check on migration. The pencil-drawn alignments of the line on maps were often tempered by the corrupt revenue staff, he writes. 'Towards the end of 1924, the local administration was found to be increasingly indulgent of the encroachments and corrupt practices.'[12] As such, the Line System had little value in restricting the movement of migrants. For instance, there was no obstacle if migrants acquired periodic *pattas* in areas not opened for their settlement.[13] Further, local resentment arose as the Assamese could not, in times of distress, indebtedness or any other pecuniary difficulty, sell or rent their lands to migrants, who generally offered relatively better prices. Such actions had, in past cases, led to the annulment of native *pattas* in many villages. In some villages, again, the principle behind the Line System had been largely dismissed, due to collusion from both communities and sympathetic views on the part of revenue authorities.[14] About the effectiveness of the Line System, Mackenzie wrote to the commissioner of the Assam Valley Division as early as 1926, 'Lines are not worth the paper they are not written on, nor when they are clearly indicated on the ground are they much more effective'.[15] Indeed, it could even be suggested that the lines were a direct stimulus to land speculators, on the principle that the nearer the line, the more valuable the land for purpose of transfer.

Yet in fact, the Lines were intended to simultaneously allow migrants to settle down peacefully and in an ordered manner, while also enabling the Assamese to either adjust or move away. And despite all of the negative ramifications, these two purposes appear to have been served—particularly with regard to wastelands, nearly all of which had been settled by 1938. Still, public opinion remained generally negative, with the migrants opposed to the system in general, while the Assamese felt the system was flouted too often. As the latter demanded a more rigid policy, Mahadev Sharma, a leading Assamese legislator, moved a resolution on 23 July 1927 with a view to prevent, or at least restrict, the settlement of wastelands by migrants from either other provinces or other countries (including the British planters).

This was followed by a heated debate in the state assembly, from which two major points emerged: first, that the scale of migration was threatening the indigenous population with fear of extinction; second, the view that the migrant was an undesirable neighbour because of his litigious nature and criminal proclivities. Sharma quoted W.C. Dundas, the Inspector-General of police, as observing that the 'immigration' had brought with it a cultured following of thieves, burglars and forgers of currency notes, who were quickly introducing 'crimes of a nature and violence hitherto unknown in this valley and with whom murder is a little more than an unfortunate incident'.[16]

While there were many arguments against migration, the opposing side was also strong, and the resolution failed by a vote of 18 to 24. All of the supporters were Hindus; while of the opponents, 12 were Muslims and the rest Europeans. But while the motion was lost, the debate carried on, and there seemed no workable solution in sight.

The publication of the Census Report of 1931 added to this fear psychosis. The Report considered this migration to be the province's most important event in the previous quarter century—an event, moreover, that in the eyes of many seemed likely to permanently alter the future of Assam, and even to destroy more effectively than did the Burmese invaders of 1820 the structure of Assamese culture and civilization. By 1936, new villages with names like Islampur, Daulatpur, Sobhanpur, Manikar *char* and Bhashanir *char* came to be established. Then-Census Commissioner C.S. Mullan's provocatively stated that Sibsagar would ultimately remain the only district where the Assamese race would find a home of its own.

False though this proved to be, Mullan's statement provided a basis to the problem which was to plague Assam henceforth'. Monirul Hussain raises a pertinent question here regarding the motives of the British colonizers: When British colonialism itself was responsible for changing the demographic profile of Assam, he asks, what was the reason behind such utterance by a colonial officer?[17] Thus, hepoints out that it was very clear that the colonial rulers wanted to patronize the social conflict between the Assamese and the migrants. It is also important to recollect that that it was at this stage that the anti-colonial struggle was attaining significant momentum in India, leading the British to follow a policy such as divide and rule—a policy that, it should be noted, paid high dividends to the colonial state. Mullan thus aimed at creating a fear psychosis among the Assamese so as to generate conflict between them and the East Bengal migrants.[18]

From the 1920s to the 1940s then, the overwhelming question in Assam's politics was whether the Line System should go or stay. The first attempt to abolish the System was made in 1936 by Khan Bahadur Nuruddin Ahmed of Nowgong, but this motion failed by a vote of seven to twenty—all seven supporters were Muslims. The second attempt was made the following year through a motion of Munnawar Ali, a prominent political leader from Sylhet. The motion was strengthened due to the active support of Abdul Matin Chowdhury, a Muslim League leader of national status. By this time, a Cabinet headed by the Muslim League leader Sir Saadullah Khan and two other members of the party had come to power in Assam, under the provincial autonomy sanctioned by the Government of India Act, 1935. The fiery speech delivered by Chowdhury on this occasion continues to stand out as a charter of the rights of the 'immigrant' Muslims in Assam, showing the sense of injustice felt at the time:

If Sir, your ancestors came to Assam with Mirzumla or Ahom kings, if you came as invaders, despoiled the population, usurped the land and settled here, you will be called an indigenous Assamese, you will be treated as the pet child, you will be shown all the favour that benign government can bestow. But Sir, if your ancestors came as pioneers, if they developed the country, if they cleared the jungle and made prosperous villages and habitable tracts, if they contributed to the development of the province, you will be treated as a pariah in your land and you will be saddled with all the difficulties and all the disadvantages that human ingenuity can invent. Sir, a more unjust, a more illogical and a more absurd system it is difficult to conceive ... a sort of vested interest is created in favour of the so-called indigenous population to the detriment of the interest of the so-called immigrants.[19]

Chowdhury repeated the specific charge that while migrants from Madras, Ranchi and elsewhere were welcome to settle in Assam, objection was raised towards the predominantly Muslim settlers from Bengal.[20] The migration question was now taking on racial and communal overtones. Just as Jinnah's 'two-nation' theory was about to be asserted, Chowdhury warned against the political effect of this policy of segregation, stating 'it closes all avenues of approach and reconciliation between the two major races inhabiting this province. The political effect of this policy is disastrous.'[21] For the first time it was openly stated that the whole question of abolition of the Line System had been taken up at the behest of the provincial Muslim League, a sentiment particularly clear in the following extract from a speech made at the state assembly by the leading politician Munnawar Ali:

> Sir, my difficulty in coming to decision was that I had a party mandate to press this resolution to division, but in the light of appeals that had been made to me repeatedly, I was thinking if it would not be better to continue the debate to the next available day so that I could in the meanwhile place the matter to the party and to have a discussion with the Hon'ble Minister of Revenue and come to a decision.[22]

Subsequently a Line System Committee was appointed in January 1938, consisting of the following members:

1.	F.W. Hockenhull	Chairman Planter
2.	Sarveswar Barua	Member Assamese Hindu
3.	Kameswar Das	Member Assamese Hindu
4.	Rabi Chandra Kachari	Member Plains Tribal
5.	Dr Mahendra Nath Saikia	Member Depressed Class
6.	Abdul Matin Chowdhury	Member Surma Valley Muslim
7.	Syed Abdur Rouf	Member Barpeta Migrant Muslim
8.	Khan Bahadur Sayidur Rahman	Member Assamese Muslim
9.	A.G. Patton	Member Revenue Secretary

The committee represented almost all political elements in Assam at the time, but it was quickly clear that little of substance would emerge from the exercise. However, the committee's eventual report brought before the province's public a few home truths regarding the ongoing migration, and today remains an important document. Though the committee was unable to prescribe a particularly workable solution, it offered unanimous agreement on some key issues:

After extensive tour in the immigrant areas and looking at the problem in all its aspects, we see no reason to modify our view that the Line System should be abolished forthwith. Our views however, were not acceptable to the majority in the committee. Holding the view, as stated above, we are prepared to consider suggestions for the modifications of the Line System as a first step to its ultimate extinction and therefore, we lent our support to the proposals for modification.[23]

The committee stated that the arguments for retention of the Line System were mainly based on the theory that once the 'immigrant' secured a foothold in a village, constant harassment compelled their Assamese neighbours to migrate elsewhere.

Letting loose of cattle in Assamese fields, cutting away

their paddy surreptitiously were cited as instances of petty harassment. Stray cases of elopement, in some case, five or ten years old, were resurrected to malign East Bengal immigrants as a class. Isolated instances of murder were ascribed to criminal propensity of the immigrants, as their racial characteristics. Grievances, real and fancied, were multiplied to buttress the case against the abolition.[24]

The report clearly stated that the whole case against the migrant as an undesirable neighbour fell to the ground in light of the fact that, all through the valley including inside the Assamese lines, these migrants were being employed as tenants or sub-tenants and *adhiars*, living in close proximity to the Assamese. 'Immigrants, it appears, are welcome as serfs to the Assamese middle class people,' the report stated, 'but are to be debarred from acquiring independent status; and the Line System [acts as a] convenient instrument for the purpose.'[25]

There was a great deal of evidence recorded in the course of the investigation carried out by the committee. Of the expert testimony included in the report, one Paines, the Deputy Commissioner of Kamrup, observed in 1938 that 'sub tenancies should be allowed if the Eastern Bengal immigrants do not build houses'.[26] Jamini Kanta Chakrabarty, the Sub-deputy Collector of Nalbari, echoed this sentiment:

'I do not see any objection to the Assamese engaging the immigrants as sub tenants or *adhidars* in areas where settlement with them is prohibited provided they are not allowed to make their houses in such areas.'[27]

In fact, the Assamese leaders continued to object to the migrants' growing control of the province's gradually receding resources. The Assamese Hindus had only just managed to get themselves close to power in the new colonial set-up, and they were not willing to give this away so fast. The bone of contention, thus, was land. The Line System was used as a statement of power, both by the English and the Assamese political leaders. For the former, it effectively divided the Hindus and Muslims; for the latter, it managed to segregate the migrants socially, and to control resource-capture by them.

MIGRANT MUSLIMS POLITICS IN ASSAM

Until 1937 the Muslims generally did not play a significant role in Assam's politics. The Indian National Congress was fast emerging as the dominant force in Assamese politics, partly because it had increasingly become the representative of the largest and politically most astute group in Assam, the Hindus, and partly because of the success of the Congress elsewhere in India. Both of these factors produced a 'bandwagon'[28] effect, with various other minority groups in Assam also joining the Congress. In fact, the Muslim community in Assam was, in the early years of the twentieth century, a socially differentiated and fragmented society broadly divided into three socially and politically exclusive groups: first, the 'indigenous' Assamese-speaking Muslims located in the Brahmaputra Valley; second, the Bengali-speaking Muslims of East Bengal origin who settled in the Brahmaputra Valley since 1911; and third, the Bengali-speaking Muslims settled in the Surma Valley (Sylhet and Cachar) since 1874.

Years of assimilation, integration, intermarriage and the resultant localization had turned the first group into an essential component of the developing Assamese nationality. The Assamese-speaking Muslims were socially more privileged and politically more integrated with the mainstream, as was amply demonstrated by their steady opposition to the migration of Muslim peasants from neighbouring East Bengal. Among the Assamese Muslims in the 1930s there was a definite trend towards concentration on specifically 'Assamese' Muslim interests. Regional Muslim conferences were held in 1934 and 1935.[29] Congress membership and involvement among Muslims were both minimal, and this detachment reflected increasing pre-occupation with the concerns of Assamese-speaking Muslims rather than interest in a broader Muslim cause.[30] For them, Bengali Muslim competition was as great a problem as the Bengali Hindus were for the Assamese Hindus.

Before the 1940s, there were significant differences between the politics of the Assamese Muslims and that of the Bengali-speaking Muslims both in the Brahmaputra, as well as the Surma Valley. The valley jealousy between the Brahmaputra and the Surma Valley Muslims precluded any chances of forming a 'Muslim' solidarity in Assam at the time. The prominent leader of the Brahmaputra Valley Muslims, Sir Saadullah Khan, often found competition in Surma Valley Muslim leaders such as Abdul Matin Chowdhury and Munnawar Ali. An example of this apathy of the Assamese Muslims toward the migrant Muslims in general was that there was considerable lobbying among the former for support for the separation of Sylhet from the province in return for a generous allocation of seats for Muslims in a Hindu-dominated Assam Valley.[31] The advantage of this would presumably be that they would be spared from Bengali Muslim competition for jobs and political opportunities, and also be able, in alliance with Assamese Hindu politicians, to politically contain the Bengali-speaking *Mymensinghia* Muslim immigrants.[32] The Delimitation Inquiry Committee in 1935 commented that 'the line of division in Assam politics is primarily not between Hindu and Muhammadan or on caste lines, but between the inhabitants of the Assam Valley and those of the Surma Valley.'[33]

Among the migrant Muslims of the Brahmaputra Valley, on the other hand, all political aims, demands and goals centred around a demand for land or the abolition of the 1920 Line System. Its leaders, such as Maulana Abdul Hamid Bhasani and Osman Ali Sadagar, were down-to-earth men who provided leadership to thousands of landless and hard-pressed migrants in the valley. Most of the migrants were peasants, and in some other cases formed a part of a teeming, landless and floating population called *utuli* in Kamrup or *wallah*[34] in Nowgong. The social composition of the community largely determined their politics.

The distance between the Assamese-speaking elite and the Bengali-speaking Muslim peasantry was often wider than the gulf separating the latter from their Hindu neighbours. The two strata of Assam's Muslim society represented two distinct streams of Muslim culture. Despite a common religion, the two communities were far apart in culture, psychological make-up and socio-economic conditions.[35] Nevertheless, the Assamese Muslims in general welcomed migrants with the hope that they would be 'Assamized' in due course, and eventually strengthen the base of Muslim communal politics in the province.[36]

In these early years, the contest for power primarily took place between the Muslim leadership of the two valleys, Brahmaputra and Surma. In the Surma Valley was the giant figure of Abdul Matin Chowdhury and also the prominent leader, later minister, Munnawar Khan, who articulated the demand for the share of the Surma Valley Muslims in political privileges within the province. There seemed to be an understanding of migrant politics being marginal even to 'mainstream' Muslim politics in Assam. This feeling percolated even through the private correspondence of Sir Saadullah Khan, who never seemed to take seriously the politics of one Maulana Bhashani, who played a key role in establishing the Muslim League in the area.[37]

Indeed, in spite of having an enormous following among the Lower Assam migrants, Bhashani failed to cut a strong, decisive figure in Assam politics.

The turning point in Assam's Muslim politics came with the setting up of the Muslim League. The Assam Pradesh Muslim League was formed in Sylhet in the late 1920s, but it never tested its principles on the platform of electoral politics until the first election to the Assam Legislative Assembly under the Government of India Act, 1935, in which four League nominees from the district made their debut. In the Brahmaputra Valley, the League had no existence at the time of elections as independents. It was Maulana Bhashani who took the initiative in establishing a branch of the League in a small village of Nowgong called Alitengri in 1938. Thus, in one stroke, Assam was linked to Muslim League politics on an all India level. In the Surma Valley, the League was founded by Abdul Matin Chowdhury, and Saadullah himself joined the League in 1940. Affiliated to the All India Muslim League in 1940, for the first time League supporters of the province as a whole were represented in their all India organization. Even more crucial for Assam was that, in the 1930s and 1940s, the Muslim League under Saadullah was able to build ministries twice, managing to stay in power until as late as 1946.

The role of Maulana Bhashani in the political mobilization of the masses of migrant Muslim peasants deserves serious analysis. Although Muslim politics was played out in the legislature by Sir Saadullah in these critical years, and though Bhashani could not really prove his astuteness in organized politics, his contribution as a grassroots-level worker among the migrants, thereby finally linking the migrant Muslim cause to greater Muslim demands, cannot be overlooked. In an analysis of the Maulana, one can draw upon the argument offered by Ahmed[38] on the role of the *mullah* in the Bengal countryside. As Ahmed demonstrated, the growth of solidarity in Bengal Muslim society was caused by a successful mobilization of rural Muslims by the *mullahs*. He further states that the average Muslim *ryot* of Eastern Bengal had a relatively more identifiable communal and religious identity than did their Hindu counterparts. Propagation of ideas among such a community was easier than in the highly stratified structure that characterized Hindu society. It was these *mullahs* who played an effective role in bridging the gap between the different sections of

Muslim population, and mobilized the masses in Bengal.

Maulana Bhashani's activities in Assam appear to be a continuation of the same trend. Ahmed had differentiated between two class of *mullahs:* the fairly well-educated *maulvis* who were relatively rare in the countryside; and the majority, the rural 'priests' who were semi-literate, with a bare knowledge of the rudiments of Islam. William Adam held the view that these individuals derived their 'support from the ignorance and superstition of the poor classes of their co-religionists.'[39] Abdul Karim, as Assistant Inspector of Schools for Muslim Education in East Bengal, wrote in 1900, 'A new line and a lucrative line has been followed by some who have assumed the dual character of the *pir* [saint] and the preacher.'[40] The rural *mullahs* ordinarily came from the rural *maktabs* or the lesser-known private *madrasas*, where they learned only the rudiments of Islamic law and ritual observances. But they were, in effect, the real leaders of the rural society, and had the power to rouse the Muslim masses to action. It was from the end of the nineteenth century that these *mullahs* began to offer political leadership to the Muslim rural masses through the institution of village *anjumans*.

The *maulana* of Bhashani, educated at a *madrasa*, taught for some time as a primary-school teacher in a village school in Kagmari, before launching his political career as a Khilafatist and non-cooperator. Amalendu Guha observes, Maulana Bhashani 'did not hesitate to exploit religious sentiments to organize and unite the province's oppressed peasants'.[41] He also noted that the 'roving Maulana with his ... great organising abilities, was accepted by the rural folk not only as a political leader but also a *pir* known to have occult powers'.[42]

Articulating the peasant demand for land, he achieved in lower Assam what the *mullahs* had achieved in Eastern Bengal—he helped to mobilize the migrant community politically, by conveying the urban message to the countryside. The economic grievances of the migrant Muslim peasantry against the Assamese Hindus could be easily manipulated to the advantage of the ambitious Muslim elite. Moreover, their grievances gradually acquired a religious dimension. But the most significant contribution of Maulana Bhashani to migrant Muslim politics was in establishing a link and merger with the broader Muslim demand for a separate state. In 1944, the

Assam Pradesh Muslim League formally took up the Muslim League cause.

Thus, though Assam's politics in the 1930s and early 1940s largely followed all-India trends, its trajectory changed considerably from the mid-1940s onwards due to its own unique two-fold political crisis. This crisis included, one, the overwhelming domination of the Sylheti Hindus in the service and social sector; and, second and more crucially, the influx of the Bengali-Muslims from East Bengal districts. The establishment of the Provincial Muslim League in Assam and the rise of communalism only deepened pre-existing faultlines in Assam's society, economy and politics. The Assamese leadership consistently felt that the solution to this situation lay essentially in two directions: the separation of Sylhet from

Assam province, and restrictions on the migration of the Bengali-speaking Muslim peasantry from other East Bengal districts into the Assamese hinterland. Both objectives were achieved when Partition finally came about in 1947.

NOTES

1. Syed Abdul Malik, *Rupaborir Polosh*, Guwahati, p. 24. (Translation from Assamese mine.)
2. See *Census of India*, Government of India, 1951.
3. Ibid.
4. *Census of India*, 1951, op. cit., p. 72.
5. Ibid., p. 72.
6. Ibid., p. 72.
7. Amalendu Guha, *Planter Raj to Swaraj: Freedom Struggle and Electoral Politics in Assam, 1826-1947*, New Delhi: ICHR, 1977, p. 205.
8. K.R. Chowdhury, Superintendent of Police, *Report of the Line System Committee (RLSC)*, vol. III: 2.
9. Ibid., Appx. 14.
10. Ibid.
11. Ibid., p. 26.
12. Guha, 1977, op. cit.
13. *RLSC*, vol. III, p. 14.
14. *RLSC*, vol. III, p. 24.
15. Ibid., Appx. 6.
16. Makhan Lal Kar, *Muslims in Assam Politics*, New Delhi: Vikas Publishing House, 1990, p. 38.
17. Monirul Hussain, *The Assam Movement, Class, Ideology, Identity*, Delhi: Manak Publications, 1993, p. 206.
18. Ibid., pp. 196-225.
19. Chowdhury, quoted in Kar, 1990, pp. 45-6.
20. Ibid., p. 46.
21. Ibid.
22. Ibid.
23. *RLSC*, vol. 1, p. 24.

24. Ibid, p. 24.
25. Ibid, p. 45.
26. *RLSC*, vol. III, p. 11.
27. Ibid, p. 14.
28. Keith Peter Ogborne, *Politics in Assam Valley, 1937-47*, unpublished thesis, Nehru Memorial Museum & Library, New Delhi, 1982, p. 232.
29. *The Statesman*, 20 November, 1934, 20 September, 1935 23-6 October 1935.
30. Ogborne, 1982, pp. 252-3.
31. *The Statesman*, 10 September 1934, 20 September 1935, 23-6 September 1935.
32. Ogborne, op. cit., p. 252.
33. Ibid., p. 253.
34. *RSLC*, vol. 1.
35. Amalendu Guha, 1977, p. 210.
36. Ibid., p. 210.
37. Sanjoy Hazarika, *The Strangers of the Mist: tales of War and Peace from India's Northeast*, New Delhi: Penguin
38. Rafiuddin Ahmed, *The Bengal Muslims, 1871 to 1906: A Quest for Identity*, Oxford University Press, 1981, p. 57
39. Governor's Resolution No. RR 36/42/4/dated 25 February 1942 & A.G. Part II, pp. 251-53.
40. Guha, op. cit., p. 281.
41. Bimal J. Dev and Dilip Kumar Lahiri, *Assam Muslims: Politics and Cohesion*, Delhi: Mittal Publications, 1985.
42. Guha, op. cit., p. 281.

CHAPTER FIVE

The July Referendum in Sylhet

The monumentous event, the 6-7 July Referendum, in which both Hindus and Muslims of Sylhet were given the opportunity to decide if their district would go to Pakistan or stay in India, is a thinly recorded chapter in Partition historiography. Much of what happened on those two fateful days of July 1947, and its subsequent impact on communities that were torn apart by the decision to partition Sylhet into two unequal parts have rarely been told before through the voices of the affected people themselves. Sixty years later, these experiences were still embedded deep in the memories of those who were present on those two days in Sylhet to cast their votes. There were others (whose voices are also captured here), who were not eligible to vote for various reasons but were present in different parts of the district on 6 and 7 July 1947.

The demographic composition of Sylhet on the eve of Partition was: North Sylhet (67 per cent

Muslim), South Sylhet (39 per cent Muslim), Sunamganj (55 per cent Muslim), Karimganj (47 per cent Muslim) and Habiganj (53 per cent Muslim). Therefore, such an outcome as happened was only to be expected in the communally charged atmosphere of the time. The result of the Referendum also reflected the religious composition of Sylhet district which was 60 per cent Muslim and 38 per cent Hindus. Moreover, several nationalist Muslims, who were part of the Jamiat-e-Ulema-e-Hind organization, voted in favour of remaining with India thus splitting the Muslim votes. From several eyewitness interviews, it also appeared that the Communist Party of India (CPI) had put in significant effort to try to influence the Referendum vote in favour of India, with the Congress and the CPI seeming to have reached an understanding of sorts.

During the course of my fieldwork in different parts of Assam and West Bengal, I noticed how the perception of the July Referendum varied between Hindus and Muslims in general which led me to present the findings on the basis of the religious affiliation of the Sylheti interviewees. In general, the Hindus supported the Congress and most Muslims put their weight behind the Muslim League, though as mentioned above, a section of the latter supported the Jamiat-e-Ulema-e-Hind. Literally, this group's name translated as the Organization of Indian Scholars, set up in 1919 and which opposed the creation of a separate Muslim state; by extension, then, those who supported the Jamiat supported the Congress's call to remain in India.

Did then Hindus and Muslims of Sylhet have different memories of the 1947 Partition? Did they respond differently to the momentous events that unfolded in July-August 1947? Not many academic works on Partition attempt to provide both sides of the story as remembered and retold by both Hindus and Muslims. Thus, the Partition storyline we inherit often happens to be just one among several competing versions of what happened, why it happened, what should have happened and most of all, who was to blame for all that happened in 1947. The version of the story we inherit depends on which community our ancestor-storytellers belonged to (in this case, Hindus or Muslims), and in what ways and to what extent Partition had impacted their own lives. Recent research has urged us to consider that there is a difference in the way people remember, or choose to remember, a process that is filtered through the prism of community. In this way, different constructs are imposed on the same reality from which differing interpretations of a historical event are likely to emerge. In the following section I try to examine and understand the different ways in which the Sylhet Referendum and Partition are remembered by Sylheti Hindus and Muslims sixty years later.

SYLHETI HINDU MEMORIES

For the most part, Hindu eyewitnesses recall the announcement of the Referendum on radio and newspapers on 21 June as coming out of the blue. Apparently, at a recent meeting of District officers it had been proposed that the Referendum be held in the second half of July because the first half of the month would usually experience heavy rainfall and floods every year. The Referendum Commissioner H.C. Stork, however, refused to allow for any delays particularly because the Viceroy Lord Mountbatten was committed to independence no later than 15 August 1947. In the days preceding the announcement there was much speculation that a Referendum might indeed be organized, but the

Hindus, most said, did not really expect this to happen. Many were 'shocked' and 'alarmed' to hear the announcement; many also recall being afraid, as they were not sure as to what such a vote might entail. Others did not even understand the implications of a Referendum on the issue of Partition. Still others thought the whole undertaking would simply be a formality, and that life would soon go back to how it had previously been. Some of the affluent Sylheti Hindu families, however, immediately moved away to other parts of Assam or West Bengal, out of fear of what could happen to them if the verdict went in favour of joining Pakistan. Some others sent the women and young children away to relatives outside Sylhet until the atmosphere returned to normal. On the other hand, many Sylheti Hindus who were living and working in other parts of Assam or India hurried back to Sylhet to cast their vote. Yet there was such little time between the 3 June announcement and the dates of the July Referendum, that many Sylheti *bhadralok* working in different parts of Assam were unable to make the trip to Sylhet to cast their votes. 'Though those two days [of Referendum] were declared as holidays by the government, yet I was unable to make the trip to Habiganj', said

Nirendra Nath Das. 'It was too rushed. They [the government] should have given us more time.'

My grandfather and the rest of the family came to know of the Referendum two or three days after the official announcement. In those days there was no electric power supply in Habiganj, in the absence of which the radio was nothing more than a showpiece in the sprawling family living room. 'We read about the Referendum in the Calcutta newspaper, which usually arrived two or three days later in Habiganj,' explained my father. His eldest brother, who was posted near Gauhati at the time, rushed back home to Sylhet as soon as he heard the announcement. This was not the best of time to travel back to the hometown, as it was the start of the monsoon season and the terrible flooding. 'But we were in a daze,' said another erstwhile inhabitant of Habiganj. 'Everything happened so fast that no one even understood what the after-effects of the Referendum might be.'

The government announced that the 1946 voters list would be followed to identify voters for the Referendum, and that people could vote any time from 9.30 in the morning to 6 in the evening on either 6 or 7 July. H.C. Stork was appointed the

Referendum Commissioner, and it was announced that he would count the votes personally and inform the Viceroy Lord Mountbatten accordingly. It was widely believed that Stork was determined to complete the business of the Referendum within the stated timeframe, and would not give in to any popular pressures for delay. 'We were given to believe that Stork was a tough guy, and petitions for a delay to a more suitable day will not be entertained by him,' confided Prasanta Chakrabarty of Habiganj.

'The election symbol for staying with India was a *ku(n)re ghar* (hut); that for joining Pakistan, a *kudal/ kuthar* (axe). When we heard the announcement of Referendum, we decided that we will not allow entire Sylhet to go!', recalled a prominent Sylheti lawyer who would play a leading role in refugee rehabilitation in Assam right after Partition. He continued:

> As a part of the Forward Bloc [political] party, we decided to bring over Sylheti Hindu voters from different parts of Assam to the voting booths. I myself brought two truckloads of voters to the Lamagaji voting booth in Sylhet Sadar [division] from Gauhati and other parts of Assam. The trucks went to Sylhet via Shillong.

The trucks accommodated some 140 individuals. A transport company based in Gauhati provided them with the vehicles, while another well-known *zamindar* paid for food and lodging for these people for close to a week in the city. The lawyer went on to describe the polling day in Sylhet:

> The journey to the polling booth was not easy. We had to cross several rivers on boats. A large number of Muslim Leaguers and National Guard Volunteers from Bihar and Uttar Pradesh tried to obstruct us in some places. A group of 10-12 men made several attempts to sink our boats. Luckily we had brought with us the zamindar's revolver. It was an empty revolver with no cartridges inside, but many of these men ran away when we brandished the revolver at them.
>
> At Lamagaji, it was a typical monsoon day. The Muslims were trying to block our way into the polling station. The volunteers were pulling the Muslims into the station first. The station was badly crowded. I think not more than 40 per cent of the Hindus could manage to vote that day. Many could not vote, though they waited long hours . . . many were pushed away, obstructed, not allowed to vote.

He remembered that 'many Muslims cast votes by force, using other people's names'. The officers-in-charge of the polling booths were Muslims as well, he said. However, a retired Assam government officer, a Sylheti himself, admitted that false votes had been cast by both Hindus and Muslims, as 'it was a fight for survival'.

A Khulna district Congress worker and participant in the campaigning immediately prior to the Referendum provides an interesting account of his personal involvement.[1] At the request of the Bengal Congress Committee, Khulna (now in Bangladesh) sent about two dozen Congress student activists to campaign in Sylhet, though most were unfamiliar with the area and none spoke the difficult Sylheti dialect. Under the guidance of the local Congress leader, Ananga Mohan Dam, they were able to paste posters in the neighbouring rural areas urging voters to support remaining with India. The day before the Referendum, however, a group of young men entered the school where the Congress workers were staying, forcibly blindfolded them, put them into a waiting lorry and drove them out of town for about 30 minutes, finally dropping them off in an uninhabited area. The workers remembered the name of the school, however, and were thus able to return safely.

In an atmosphere of such distrust between communities, it did not help that the Referendum was hastily pushed through. Even confusion about what such a move meant sometimes gave rise to greater worries and uncertainties among the people. Young

Hindu men walked around the streets in groups singing 'Your hut is calling you, my friend' (*Tomar-e daak-e tomar ghar, bondhu re*).[2] Muslim youths, on the other hand, went around warning 'We will break the hut with the axe' (*Kuthar diya ghar bhangbo*).[3]

'It was as if the quiet and friendly Muslim workers had been transformed overnight,' said Sashidhar Sengupta, a well-known lawyer whose *desher baari* was in Sylhet, and who had returned two days before the Referendum to cast his vote. 'There was a marked confidence in the way they walked and spoke those days. But we, the Hindu landowners, had not treated them very well in the past, either. The tables being turned on us now.'[4] He went on to describe how his wife wept endlessly, and wanted to go to Shillong to stay with her eldest brother until life returned to normal in Sylhet. The day that she did finally leave for Shillong turned out to be the last time ever she saw her home in Sylhet—it was her husband who eventually had to join her in Shillong, instead. Later, the entire family moved to Gauhati and built a new house. Before that, though, Sengupta's most vivid memory of the Referendum was the incessant rain: 'There was waterlogging all around my house. I had to roll up my pants and carry my shoes in my hand as I walked through the mud and water. But I was determined to vote.'

In an incomplete article, Digindra Chandra Datta describes the rainy season in the rural areas of Sylhet:

> Our land is made of river-clay; that's why the land is very soft . . . huge tracts of land go under water during the monsoon season. Whichever direction you look at, there is water everywhere. From the distance, it looks like some houses are floating on the water . . . you can barely see anything else besides floating rooftops. When the loud, powerful winds create waves on the water, and the waves crash loudly on houses, it sounds like sea-waves.[5]

In such a situation, asked Rabindranath Choudhuri, formerly of Habiganj, 'How did the government expect us to vote during the monsoons?' The government, on its part argued that 'circumstances have compelled the holding of the referendum at a time when a huge part of the district is flooded and a substantial percentage of polling stations will be in the flooded areas. Voters will have to find their way to them as best as they can'.[6] The only help the government 'can give them is not to indent upon local transport for its own requirement'.[7]

However, Choudhuri continued:

Why couldn't they wait for a month at least? Why did they organize it in the rainy season? Did they want us to lose? People started gathering together in small groups in their homes and discussed the future. What would happen to them if Sylhet indeed was lost to East Pakistan? All those who had relatives in Assam were the lucky ones . . . they had a place to go to and start a new life.

Many of the voters came to the polling booths by boat and others by bus or on foot. Even though there was no major violence in Sylhet like in other parts of Bengal or Punjab, Choudhuri said,

the Hindus knew that one day or the other they would have to leave because the communal feelings would not go away so easily. Both communities had shown that they distrusted each other, and that was not a good start. But unlike the Muslims who stayed back in India, we left in entire families. Luckily we did not suffer from broken families like the Muslims afterwards.

Some reacted immediately to this changing in relationship between communities. Shudhangshu Nandy said that he lost his desire to vote in the Referendum when he saw 'the changed relations between Hindus and Muslims in Sylhet, my own land. . . . They were our own people.' Nandy said he was disturbed to see the change in the attitude of the Muslims of his neighbourhood. 'They used to be so docile and friendly. Now it seems that they were getting ready for a confrontation of some sort.' He remembered walking down the road in front of his house in the evenings a few days before the Referendum.

> The roads were waterlogged, so I had to walk carefully. In the nearby tea shop, a group of Muslim boys were drinking tea and directing comments at the Hindu people passing by. I could not pretend that I did not hear them because I had to walk very slowly through the water. They laughed loudly when one of my shoes got stuck in the mud and I had to walk back with the shoe in my hand. It disturbed me a lot. I stopped going out for the next few days.

At first, Nandy refused to vote on the day of the Referendum; it was only through the efforts of his brothers that he was convinced to go to the polling booth. He still remembers the intimidating comments made by the Muslim League workers when he and his brothers were entering the booth. 'I knew right at that moment that Sylhet was no longer ours. It seemed that we had already lost even before the Referendum,' he sighed. 'And I was proven right in less than a week's time.'

Narendra Dattagupta, himself the son of an optee, pointed out that the communal atmosphere in Sylhet had indeed heated up 'suddenly and in a very short time'. Both the Muslim League and the Congress had only a few weeks in which to campaign before the Referendum. 'Perhaps the Sylhet Muslims felt that they had to jump into campaigning from day one; their leaders were well organized and focussed,' Dattagupta said. 'The Hindus like us were too scared to campaign openly; moreover, our leaders were nowhere to be seen.' He also pointed out that just before and immediately after the Referendum, the Hindus felt particularly vulnerable because many of the well-to-do among them had already begun to migrate out of Sylhet in anticipation of trouble. 'My father would often tell us that, after they [the rich and prominent Hindus] left, he began to feel insecure . . . as if the umbrella above his head had been snatched away in the midst of heavy rains. He did not feel safe anymore.' Several others said that the Hindus were beginning to feel apprehensive long before the Referendum was organized primarily because of their numerical minority, and lack of political organization.

On 7 July 1947, the *Sadiniya Asamiya* newspaper reported that it had rained continuously for the two days leading up to the Referendum. However, until

2 p.m. on the day of the poll there was no news of any untoward incident, nor did any such news come from the Sylhet Referendum office. 'But there were scuffles and cases of intimidation all over,' said Sashidhar Sengupta.

> People gathered together on the evenings of the 6 and 7 of July, and talked until midnight. The question on everyone's lips was, 'What will happen if . . . ?' I think we were even afraid to say the word *Partition* in case it came true! My mother would go around passing food to everyone, and the only words to come out of her mouth were 'Dugga-Dugga' [chanting the name of the goddess, Durga]. It was a time of such uncertainty all around us!

But Sengupta himself admitted that he did not come across any case of violence anywhere in Sylhet town. Eventually, however, there was news of one incident from Sunamganj, and it was heard that women voters had faced some problems in voting centres. After the first day of voting, Congress politician Rohini Kumar Choudhury, then the finance minister of Assam, also claimed that many Hindus living in Muslim-dominated villages were not being allowed to vote, and he pledged that any Hindu who could not vote on the 7th would be escorted to the poll booths on the 8th by the military. The following day, the *Sadiniya Asamiya* reported the sound of gunshots during the voting, and it appeared that one person had died from firing by military personnel. On 9 July, it was announced that vote counting would continue for another five days, until the 14th, at the bungalow of the district commissioner of Sylhet. On 12 July, the governor of Assam, Sir Akbar Hydari, and some government officers stated that the law-and-order situation in Sylhet had not been disturbed during the vote counting. 'These press reports are fantastic and entirely false. Perfect peace and order is prevailing in the district',[8] he commented. However, accusations of foul-play and malpractices by both sides during the Referendum kept on pouring in. 'Some of the common concerns of the Hindus was the obstructions to the polling booths and impersonations by League supporters', said Sukumar Sen. Hydari on the other hand stated that the Assam premier, and he and the officers felt that 'the wildly irresponsible statements given to the press by Basanta Kumar Das and other Bengali workers were due to their realisation that they were losing the battle and so provide an explanation in advance of their defeat'.[9]

SYLHETI MUSLIM MEMORIES

In the days leading up to the Referendum, people in different parts of Sylhet would meet to discuss and debate almost everywhere, in the streets, at homes or in shops. At the national level, it was known that India was going to get independence from the British, and there was much tension among both Hindus and Muslims in Karimganj as to whether Sylhet would remain with India or go to Pakistan. In the neighbouring Maulanabazar area, all Muslims wanted to vote for Pakistan; but in Karimganj, many Muslims wanted to remain with India.[10] Kayum Mia of Patherkandi area in Karimganj, for instance, could not remember when it was that he first heard the announcement for the Referendum, but he could remember that many Muslims were praying at mosques and at home that *Aamra Pakistan chai* (We want Pakistan), while Hindus were rushing to the village temples to pray to stay with India.[11]

Adbus Shukkur Khan[12] could not remember either the exact date when the news of the Referendum was officially announced on the radio, but he remembered that he was a student at the government high school in Karimganj at the time. The student community around him felt as though something 'great and big was going to happen'. Though people had heard of a Referendum being held in the North West Frontier Province (NWFP), on the other side of the subcontinent, it was a largely unfamiliar idea and many were confused about what it would mean for their community.[13]

Nazimuddin Ahmed had only heard about the Referendum almost a week after the formal announcement on 21 June 1947. He was apprehensive because some of his neighbours said that there might be some communal clashes or riots during the voting, while some others had said that the whole exercise was a 'British conspiracy'.[14] People in Karimganj immediately began speculating about where the Partition lines would fall, and whose lands would fall on which side. There was such little time between the announcement and the holding of the Referendum that people did not have enough time to make any plan other than to go with the flow.[15] Ahmed's father was worried that they might be separated from some close relatives who lived in different parts of Sylhet district. What if his land fell in Pakistan and theirs in India, or the other way around? Could brothers be divided by borders? But on the whole, Ahmed said, there was excitement and expectation all around, because they understood and supported Jinnah's call for Sylhet to be included in East Pakistan.[16] The Referendum was the first step towards the fulfilment of that hope.

Moinuddin Choudhury[17] remembered that when his family heard the news of the Referendum, they thought 'it was like a general election'. Most did not understand what exactly was to take place until the political leaders explained it to them. *Apnara kudal-re vote diba* (You must vote for the axe), they would advise.[18] His own father was an *imam* in the local mosque but also an enthusiastic supporter of the Jamiat-e-Ulema-e-Hind. As such, it was a time of hard decision for the family. Though many of their friends and relatives urged them to support the cause for East Pakistan because 'it is the better choice for Muslims', his father decided to support the Jamiat's call to remain in India instead. As a supporter of the Muslim League, Badruddin Laskar, on the other hand, hoped that Karimganj would go to East Pakistan after the Referendum.[19]

Nizamuddin Ahmed's village was a part of the four *thanas* where the Referendum was to be held.[20] He too could not remember the exact date or time when he first heard the announcement, but at the time he must have been about 25 years old. He was a schoolteacher for two years before Partition, and along with other locals he was eagerly waiting for the Referendum in order to vote for Pakistan. 'We were almost sure that these parts of the Sylhet district would go to Pakistan', he said.

Still others did not want the vote to go forward at all, including, as noted earlier, due to rumours of British conspiracy. Abdul Rashid recalled that just after the declaration of the Referendum, one British man was shot dead near Kushiara River and, out of fear for her life, his daughter too jumped into the river. 'Some angry Muslim people were searching for the British person,' he said, 'as they thought declaration of Referendum was a conspiracy of the British officials.'[21]

When the Referendum was finally held on the rainy mornings of 6 and 7 July, people were afraid that 'anytime, anything may happen', according to Abdul Rashid.[22] A large team of Muslim League leaders and workers came from Bengal, under the leadership of Hossain Suhrawardy. All over Bengal, Muslims were saying *Chalo, Sylhet chalo* (Let's go to Sylhet), and the Muslim League workers had even penetrated into the remotest of villages, the rains and flood waters notwithstanding.[23] Large numbers of members of the Muslim National Guards also came to Sylhet from Bengal to assist in the campaigning. According to Rahman Mahmud Ansari,

> They [the Muslim leaders] were so fired up, and they really tried to convince the people that they should vote for Pakistan because there was no future for them in India. Perhaps the League workers were afraid that their task would be uphill since both Congress and Jamiat were both supporting the call for India. Some feared the Assam government could influence the outcome of the Referendum because the polling officers were all government employees. My father's friend also suspected that some powerful Hindu and British officials may play a role in the outcome, and manage to keep Sylhet with India.[24]

Some Congress volunteers, along with young Sikh supporters, also travelled to interior areas to campaign for India. 'During the campaign period we would hear new complaints every day', said Fazlul Hussain.[25] 'Today the League would point a finger at the Congress, and tomorrow the Congress would complain against the League workers.' Further, not everyone was eligible to vote, with eligibility based on the Chowkidari system, or possession of some amount of landed property. Therefore, some families had far more or fewer eligible voters.

On both days of the Referendum, Muslim League supporters walked around the Karimganj town area waving flags and chanting emotional slogans. 'The League's campaigning was worth seeing, as they spoke in loudspeakers from beautifully decorated vehicles and boats', Hussain recalled.[26]

> The Congress party workers too were busily mobilizing support, but they were fewer in number, and their campaign not so eye-catching. I remember them saying that the 'hut' was a sign of unity, and the 'axe' was a sign of violence or threat, which made me a little angry.

There were 239 polling booths in all, each with two presiding officers and several polling officers. A large number of officials were also kept aside for the counting of ballots, which was supposed to be completed within two days though it took far longer.

Abdul Shukkur recalled that polling was conducted in the Mahaganj Pathsala situated to the north of his village. Even on the day of voting, he said, people were unsure as to what they were expected to do, and so generally followed the instructions of the senior community and political leaders. As a youngster, he remembered going to see the Referendum with his friends 'as if it was a festival'. Indeed, the number of spectators was perhaps more than the number of actual voters, with schoolchildren running around waving Muslim League flags and others were waving Congress party flags.[27] Observers crowded around to watch voters streaming into the booths in two separate lines: one for the *ghar* and the other for the *kudal*.

Hafiz Matin wanted to cast his vote too, but was prevented from doing so due to 'some disorder', fights or quarrels, in the area. But he remembered that his father voted in favour of the Muslim League. Likewise, when both of Abdul Latif's parents voted, he vaguely recollected some 'scuffles' taking place at the polling booth, as well as in the neighbourhood—quarrels, hurling stones at each other, etc.—though there were not many such incidents. He also remembered hearing statements such as, 'If you want to be a good Muslim, support the Muslim League; if you want to be a patriot, support the Congress.' However, he personally believed that 'religion had a more powerful impact on people, and so almost all Muslims were with the Muslim League'.

Murakib Ali had himself voted at the Referendum in favour of Pakistan. At the time of the Referendum, he was living with his uncle in East Bengal, but his father asked him to return to Karimganj to cast his vote. His was a village with a mixed population of Muslims, Hindus, Manipuris and some fishermen castes. Some Muslim families were divided between supporters of both the Muslim League and the Congress party. While Abdul Noor also voted, his family members were all supporters of the Jamiat, and he still remembered the uncertainties of the time, with many people wondering whether they had made the right choice. 'People were in general perplexed as to what would happen if we were to go to India or Pakistan, or whichever area we would be going to— or, if there would be Pakistan, where its lines would fall', he said.[28] Many of his relatives in the border areas anticipated that they might remain with India.

With many people simultaneously excited and worried, the problem was that 'it was a blind man's game', said Monir Sheikh. 'We had no idea of the technicalities and no power to stop the outcome even if we did not agree with it.'[29] Even neighbours started looking at each other with suspicion. 'We averted our eyes when we saw our Hindu neighbours, who also looked unhappy to see us', Sheikh recalled. 'What happened to years of living together? Our parents stopped the younger children from playing with the neighbours' children. It is only for a short while', they said. 'After Partition everything will be fine.'[30]

Supporters of both the Jamiat and the Congress were confident that the decision would be in their respective favour. The Congress workers would go around saying, 'Don't go to East Bengal [Pakistan], don't die of hunger' (*Purba Bang-e jaiyo na, anahare moriyo na*).[31] The Muslim League, on the other hand, mobilized support by saying 'If you vote for the axe, then the rest of your lives you can live in peace. We will give you freedom' (*Aapnara jadi kudal-e vote diyen, tahole shara-ta jibon araam korbaye. Aamra apnader-ke mukti dibo*).

Saifunissa was born at Sutarkandi in Karimganj. She was generally uninterested in politics until the Referendum was announced, and even then she was not quite sure of what was taking place. Her husband ran a grocery shop in Karimganj town, and she remembers casting her vote along with her husband and parents-in-law. As her village was on the border, there was an equal mix of Hindus and Muslims in her neighbourhood. Muslims were shouting *Allahu akbar!* (God is great) while Hindus chanted the name of Lord Ram in the streets. Women were given strict instructions to stay inside their homes, while men went around only in groups.[32]

Saifunissa admitted that, as a woman, she was expected to vote for whichever side her husband asked her to favour. In Saifunissa's case, her husband asked her to vote for Pakistan, and she obeyed without any hesitation. For the womenfolk, especially Muslims, it was not a matter of major concern, she said, as they were generally not involved in politics. She repeatedly said that her husband and father-in-law did a 'great deal of good work' to connect Sylhet with East Pakistan. In fact, when her father-in-law heard that Karimganj was to remain with India, he was so devastated that he did not eat anything for days.

Taibunissa had a similar story to tell. People were largely ignorant about the Referendum, especially the women, she confirmed. She heard about the Referendum only when her husband asked her to vote in favour of Pakistan. Before that, all she knew was that 'something big was going to happen', and that because it was very serious they needed to support their husbands. She recalled only feeling that the Hindus were trying to do something wrong:

My husband and father-in-law were very busy those days. They would be out of the house all day. They would come home only to eat, and would be angry if the rice was not cooked by then. All we women knew was that the men are doing something sacred [*pabitra*]. One day we were told that the next morning we would have to wake up early and go out to save the Muslim people. The Muslims wanted to go to Pakistan. Later we came to know that it was the day of the Referendum. We women did not go out much those days, so we came back quickly after casting votes. The children went running to the polling booths to see what was happening. We were a bit worried but later my husband came back and told me that there were no problems. 'Our prayers,' he said, 'will soon be answered and we will all go to Pakistan.'[33]

Unfortunately for Taibunissa's husband, the Boundary Commission left four *thanas* of Karimganj sub-division of Sylhet within India, though not without some initial fumbling and the rise of wild rumours.

The day after the Referendum, Taibunissa recalled, 'people happily believed that their voice had been heard, and Pakistani flags were hoisted here and there'.[34] Muhammad Gyasuddin remembers seeing military men roaming the streets, especially in the border areas. One of them offered him a biscuit, which he took, but his *dadu* (grandfather) scolded him as he did not want to take anything from a non-Muslim. The young Gyasuddin had to purify himself by taking a quick dip in a pond. Women continued to stay at home, as most believed it was unsafe for them to go out because there were so many soldiers all around. Gyasuddin could remember that both Muslim League and Congress supporters continued to shout loud slogans in the streets. In particular, the former widely distributed sweets while jubilantly waving their flags. For the first two or three days, many believed the rumours going around: that Karimganj had become a part of East Pakistan, and 'great celebrations were started'.[35]

There were also some instances of stone-throwing at supporters of the Jamiat.[36] Abdus Shukkur Khan recalled his father being beaten up by some League supporters, and his own right arm being slightly injured. Later, people were told that Karimganj had been divided between India and East Pakistan based on some 'administrative convenience'.[37] For the next two days there were loud pro-India cries of *Vande Mataram*, *Ram-Krishna* and *Bharat Mata* reverberating around the town. But suddenly the government changed the 'decision' the people thought had been made, said Moni Hossain, and announced that the preliminary vote-counting had been wrong. A fresh result was made public, which stated that Karimganj was to remain within India because 'the Congress and the Jamiat had won these four *thanas*'.[38]

When the Indian flags went up after this announcement there was further confusion, and no one knew what was going to happen next. Pakistani flags were burnt and Indian flags were hoisted everywhere. Taibunnisa's husband and others were depressed, but they had no option but to accept the verdict—Taibunnisa's husband told her that they would have to accept the 'cruel truth' that now they would have to live in India. Her family still had the grocery shop, and she remembered that some Hindu boys quickly pasted papers on top of the pictures of axes from before the Referendum. People were speaking about Partition for many days, but for most of the women, she said, it did not create much sensation:

> We were strictly ordered to stay inside our houses . . . our village had people of the other community . . . and our male members protected us. Even when we were to go to pond, someone used to be at our home. We were afraid.[39]

Many people decided to leave for Pakistan, especially those who had been officers in government jobs. Many Hindus also came to the area as optees, while some others exchanged land with their Muslim counterparts. As a result, the Hindu population increased in Karimganj town. Tafajjul Ahmed believed that 'virtually nobody was interested in this part of the then Sylhet. Even the Muslim League was not so interested'. For the Muslim League, Ahmed said, *Paile bhalo aslo, na paileo hoibo. Baki jaga to ase Sylheter lage jeta Pakistan-e pore* (It is good if they get it, but even if they don't get it does not matter much. There are many other areas of Sylhet that have gone to Pakistan). The Assamese leadership wanted to get rid of all of Sylhet, in order to prove its majority in the state, he said, suggesting that the central leadership was overburdened with other areas—in order to include Agartala with India, the sentiments of many Muslim Sylhetis were not considered.[40]

When the results were first announced, the Muslim supporters of Jamiat were upset because it looked like the League had won. The League supporters, said Abdul Noor,

> humiliated the Congress supporters, especially the Muslims. They asked us to wash the cups and plates that they left

after drinking tea. Most of the Maulavis were backing the Jamiat. So the League supporters said, *Mullar pithit lekia dibo je ekhon kar lage thakbai . . . tumra amrare thagiso. . .* [We will write on the shoulders of the Mullahs, who will you live with now? You have betrayed us]. They would tease and humiliate us. *Amrar abastha biralor moto hoislo* [Our condition had become like cats]. But when Indian flag was hoisted after three days, everyone became silent. It was our day. We won and became a part of India.[41]

In those days immediately after Referendum, the Jamiat supporters found it particularly difficult to face Muslims who were League supporters. In fact, many felt that their condition had become even worse than the Hindus after the Referendum, feeling that they had been 'humiliated and defeated in the eyes of our own people'.[42] Moreover, during the two days of the Referendum, they claimed that the League supporters had physically tried to stop them from entering polling booths, particularly in the Aushkandi centre. The presiding officers, they said, could do little in the face of League intimidation. Once the second announcement was made, *Jamiat-er kase nutan jaan ailo. Ekhon amrar shomoy* (It was as if the Jamiat had got a new life. This was our time now).[43] Now the condition of the League supporters had become like *bhija biral*—literally, like a 'wet cat', referring to a dispirited or mortified state of mind.[44]

A total of 239,619 votes had been cast for joining East Pakistan, and 184,041 votes for remaining in Assam/India. On 30 July 1947, the Boundary Commission for Bengal was set-up in order to determine the path and direction of the borders of Sylhet. The four Indian members of the Commission were Justice Bijan Bihari Mukherjee and Justice Charu Chandra Biswas representing the Congress and Justice Abusaleh Muhammad Akram and Justice Fazlur Rahman representing the Muslim League. Once the borders of Bengal were decided upon, the Commission invited representations by all interested parties in the Sylhet question. Open sittings were organized in Calcutta on 4-6 August 1947. Claims and counter-claims were put forward by the Muslim League as well as the Sylhet District Congress Committee and the Hindu Mahasabha (an organization for Hindu unity).

One of the contentious issues was the future of Sylhet's sizeable non-Muslim population of tea-garden labourers from Central India (who had not been allowed to vote for being no more than a floating population), as well as Sylhet's non-Muslim majority thanas. These areas, it was argued, should be included on the Indian side as the Partition was to be decided on the basis of religion. In a joint memorandum, the groups argued that since non-Muslims constituted 39.3 per cent of Sylhet's population, at least 2,140 of the total 5,444 sq. miles should be given to them.[45] It made an emphatic plea for taking the river Kushiara as the northern boundary between the two dominions of (East) Pakistan and India.[46] The Muslim League, on the other hand, demanded that the entire district be given to East Pakistan. The Commission members were themselves initially unsure if the Commission had the jurisdiction to detach from Assam any Muslim-majority area that was contiguous to East Bengal or was limited to only those within Sylhet district and areas contiguous to Sylhet.

Sir Cyril Radcliffe, the chairman of the Commission, finally held the latter view as official. Accordingly, he recommended the transfer of most of Sylhet district—barring a small Hindu pocket of about 700 sq. miles, with a population of a little over two million—to East Pakistan, an area that included 12 *thanas*, including those of Ratabari, Karimganj, Patherkandi and Badarpur. The results were submitted to the Viceroy on 13 August; it was not published until 17 August. This led to confusion as it was believed that based on the Referendum results, the entire district of Sylhet had been handed over to East Pakistan on 14 August. Three days afterwards it was clarified that the three-and-a-half *thanas* of Ratabari, Badarpur, Karimganj and Patherkandi were to be returned to India.

Few of the people I interviewed had heard the announcement on 14 July because not many possessed radios and many others did not have electricity in their homes. Osman Ali Khan of Karimganj was delighted with the outcome, or what many Sylhetis mistakenly believed to be the outcome for two whole days after 15 August. 'All this time we had been praying to join Pakistan; our prayers were finally answered. We were so happy!' Khan's happiness, however, proved to be short-lived as only two days later it was announced that 12 *thana*s had been retained in Assam due to administrative reasons. Karimganj, on the border of Assam, was one of the areas to remain with India. The Muslims who had voted for India heaved a sigh of relief. 'For those two days, we had been treated like traitors by our fellow Muslims', said Shajahan Mohammed. 'Now we felt safe.' Eventually, however, only the three and a half *thanas* of Ratabari, Karimganj, Patharkandi and Badarpur were retained by the government of Assam.

VIOLENCE IN SYLHET: HINDU AND MUSLIM TESTIMONIES

Before Partition, Nazimuddin Ahmed had two homes, one in Sylhet town and another in Karimganj, the latter of which belonged to his maternal grandparents. Along with his parents and other siblings he had lived in Sylhet town during his childhood, but soon after he turned 20 his family moved to Karimganj. On the day of Referendum, he was in Karimganj with his parents, and he could remember his uncles telling him about some instances of violence near their Sylhet home. After the declaration of Partition, he could remember seeing people coming from East Pakistan to Assam, 'swimming along the River Kushiara', most of whom were Sylheti Hindus. However, he could only remember one incident of communal violence in his village (which was eventually divided between India and Pakistan) during the Referendum period. As his home was in the border area, he and some friends formed a village committee to guard the village. 'Near the Kushiara, just after Referendum, there was a clash between Hindus and Muslims, both of whom were carrying stones and bamboo sticks.' He with some others stood between the two groups, and stopped them from attacking each other. But there were no other major communal clashes in Karimganj until after Partition, at which time the 'lives of many people [were] destroyed along with their property'.

Gyasuddin's family, meanwhile, was socially boycotted by their Muslim friends when it was known that his father had voted in favour of the 'hut'. But there were no instances of intimidation or violence against him or his family. Likewise, there were no riots or clashes in his neighbourhood, though a few shops were burnt down in Karimganj.[47] Eyewitnesses from Hailakandi (a Muslim-majority area in neighbouring Cachar) said that there were no riots there, either,[48] nor in Neelambazar[49] or Chandkhira.[50] Taibunissa could remember some Hindus attacking their grocery shop, though she was not aware of any other violent incident.[51] At Maizdhi (in the Settlement neighbourhood of Karimganj), some minor incidents took place during the Referendum, including quarrels and stone-throwing; but otherwise there were no major conflicts at that time.[52] Indeed, almost all rural areas were free from conflict during the voting period.[53]

Though Murakib Ali did not hear about any communal rioting in the neighbouring areas, many people believed that some violence indeed took place in Karimganj town and in East Pakistan generally, in the aftermath of the declaration of Partition. 'As the Patherkandi area [where his home was located] is away from the East Pakistan border, instead closer to Tripura, no such after-effect of violence could be seen there. We just heard some rumours', he said.[54] His testimony was corroborated by Kayum Mia, who also lived in Patherkandi at the time of Partition and who agreed that 'there was no violent situation' in his neighbourhood, though he and one of his brothers were reprimanded and even beaten up by some Jamiat supporters in one instance.[55]

The real effect of Partition, however, could only be seen during the 1950 riots in Karimganj town, when 'many Hindus migrated from East Pakistan'.[56] The situation deteriorated as these Hindus brought back with them many tales of the suffering they had experienced in East Pakistan, and their arrival caused considerable bitterness among the Muslims in Karimganj. Kayum Mia remembered that in and around 1949-50, in a place called Baraigram, a few kilometres from Patherkandi, *Train khara karia mara pita, galagali hoislo manusher majhe* (People stopped trains, beat up and yelled at each other). After that incident, many Muslims decided to leave for East Pakistan. In such a tense atmosphere, Mia recalls, many Hindus would shout from the roads, *Tumra muslim-ra Pakistane jao . . . Amrare tumra shesh karla . . . Ekhon amra tumrarke khatia shesh karbo . . . taratari desh charo!* (You Muslims go to Pakistan. You all have finished us. Now we will cut you up and finish you. Leave the country quickly).

Abdul Jalil could also remember clashes among Hindus and Muslims in 1950. Both communities were clearly apprehensive about losing their rights, and harboured ill feelings caused by many earlier political events. 'It caused a sharp division among people', Jalil said. 'And even though we are part of Assam, we are not getting any help from the state today. So it would have been better if we did not have Partition, or we should have been in the Bengali dominated area of East Pakistan.'[57] Abdul Rashid had himself participated in some of the communal clashes. He said, 'People used to go to the riots wearing *kerosiner container er tin katia bukut bandhia*—tying sheets of tin cut from kerosene containers on the chest—or *gua gacher bakol paria*, wrapping the bark of the betel-nut tree around the body. One of his good friends, Ramdas, who was a Hindu, died in the riots.[58]

Though the Referendum took place relatively peacefully, 'the division between the two communities was created more by the Partition', said Tafajjul Ahmed.[59] Many Hindus fled the riots in East Pakistan in 1950 and came to India, he continued, and 'They obviously did not have a good image of Bengali Muslims, and a sense of hatred existed in their minds.' The local Muslims, said Ahmed, 'those who were still here, or had decided not to go to Pakistan, now had to bear the responsibility of the actions of those Muslims in Pakistan who were financially much better off'. He believed that, through no fault of their own, many innocent Muslims lost their lives in the riots of 1950, with many Muslim houses torched in the riot-torn areas of Karimganj town, Hailakandi and Silchar. 'Though there is no such open clash today [between the two communities], yet no community can easily forget its past', he said.

From all available oral accounts, Hailakandi was the worst affected area in 1950. Abdul Matin also did not remember any violence before or at the time of the Referendum. But after Independence the violence did finally come, in the 1950s and again in the 1960s. Matin could remember one high-profile incident in 1950 in which a Muslim man was cut into pieces by some Hindus, but he could not remember the exact reason why. Either way, this led to more communal riots, due to Muslim retaliation. One of his sisters was pregnant at that time, and he recalled that on the day of his nephew's birth everyone was tense, as his sister's husband was yet to come home from Karimganj where he worked. The sensational murder had led to a situation of terror, in which no one knew what was going to happen.

Taibunissa remembered that 'several years after the Partition, people were frightened by the 1950 riots in the town area'. Many houses were burnt, people were afraid to open up their shops, and their own grocery shop too was closed for many days at that time. 'Muslim people stopped buying from Hindus and vice versa', she said. 'Earlier, Hindu women talked to us; but after the riot we women were more confined to the houses.' Indeed, these were times like nothing before.

As outlined in the previous section, from most available sources as well as fieldwork among first- and second-generation Partition migrants in the Brahmaputra and Barak valleys, it would appear that there was no major incident of violence in Sylhet before or right after the Referendum of 1947. That is not to say, however, that there were no cases of petty criminal activity, robbery or even small-scale attacks on villages soon after the result of the Referendum was announced. The *Census of India* for 1951 noted that, at the time of the Partition, Assam largely escaped 'degrading and inhuman occurrences', though 'it could not do so for all the time'. It speaks of the 'inevitable repercussions' of the riots and communal massacres in other parts of the country, which led to 'some atrocities [in Sylhet], which, however, were insignificant compared with those which occurred elsewhere'.[60] It does note, however, that in February and March 1950, there were widespread communal disturbances in the Assam districts of Cachar, Goalpara, Kamrup, Nowgong, Darrang and Tripura, followed by a very heavy influx of refugees.[61]

Haimanti Roy mentions an attack on the village of Kaibarta in Sylhet by Muslims on 11 February 1948, which caused 'substantial economic damage but no loss of human lives'.[62] She also notes that several written complaints were sent by Sylheti Hindus demanding resettlement in Assam, citing communal threat and forcible conversions to Islam. Upon investigation, the East Pakistan inspector-general of police found such allegations to be 'maliciously false', and suggested that people were migrating to India not because of torture by Muslims but because 'they are at heart deadly [*sic*] against Pakistan'.[63] Roy also notes that East Pakistani officials regularly suggested that the primary basis for migration and new citizenship was economic benefits on the other side, rather than minority persecution in East Pakistan. The *Census of India* for 1951 too notes that it is not unlikely that 'some people being needy cross over from Sylhet to India, in order to avail themselves of the benefit of rehabilitation conferred by the government and thus temporarily swell the number of refugees'.[64]

It cannot be denied, however, that a major factor for migration was the psychological pressure, or perceived fear, of what would happen to their families if they remained in East Pakistan. According to many reports, a feeling of fear gripped both communities, and both Hindus and Muslims began to move around in public 'in groups of six or ten'.[65] Many Hindus were particularly swayed by stories and rumours of the atrocities that were taking place against Hindus in Punjab,[66] with many others worried that their religion, culture and self-respect would not be safe in Pakistan.[67] Indeed, every new incident of violence against Hindus elsewhere in Punjab or Bengal gave a push to fresh out-migration into Assam from neighbouring East Bengal districts. While there were no cases of outright violence in Sylhet, Tarun Datta, a physician from south Sylhet said,

> the wind was hot with speculation, tension and fear, and different people said different things. But by the next day [15th July] almost everyone knew of the result. We were shocked when the reality dawned on us, though we were expecting the outcome. It was very difficult for us to accept, but we had no choice. I did not want to leave my home.

Though many others like him did not want to leave Sylhet, it was only a matter of time before they changed their minds. 'We heard so many stories coming out of Punjab . . . we were so afraid. It is true that nothing major happened in Sylhet, but we were not sure for how long we would be safe here.' Salil Dattaroy, a retired school-teacher now settled in Kolkata, remembered the *shukriya* or thanksgiving procession that the Muslim League supporters had organized a couple of days after the announcement of the Referendum results. 'I knew we had to leave now. Our time was up', he said 'But one good thing was that [after the referendum] even the Hindu leaders of Sylhet took out a small procession in the spirit of communal harmony. I think that is why we did not face major riots and killings like in other parts of East Bengal, or Punjab.' Thus, over the next few years, a large number of Sylhetis, including my grandfather, left their ancestral land and homes, and travelled across the newly-drawn borders to build new homes in a new country.

The tension in Sylhet following the Referendum and Partition was felt by all quarters. In particular, the positions of the Sylheti Hindus and the nationalist Muslims belonging to the Jamiat-e-Ulema-e-Hind became doubly staked, as their participation in the Referendum had exposed their reluctance to be part of Pakistan. A senior Assam government official (now retired and living in West Bengal) who at the time of Partition was a young man living in Sylhet, said that the daily news-paper *Azad*, published from Calcutta and widely circulated in Sylhet, added fuel to the situation by publishing inflammatory articles about what was taking place in Sylhet as well as in Kashmir. In addition, 'public lectures and provocative discussions' broadcast on radio created a sense of panic among Hindus in Sylhet. Eventually, the tension led many to decide that they would have to move.

One eyewitness in Silchar said that after the Referendum it was only he and his brother who had migrated. His parents, he said, had no desire to leave their birthplace, as they were well-placed people in Sylhet. He also spoke of other friends who, likewise, had initially decided not to migrate, but did eventually move out of fear. It appears that once the upper-caste, middle-class Hindu leaders began to migrate to India, the lower castes and classes too began to move due to increased feelings of insecurity and apprehensions over potential violence. One Sylheti eyewitness writes that the main reason why his family stayed back in Sylhet even after the Referendum was due to his 'dream to be a . . . student of the famed Murari Chand (MC) College in Sylhet.'

It was only with the utmost reluctance that he finally decided to move to Calcutta with the rest of his family members—though he remained unimpressed by the colleges there.[68]

Thus, outright physical violence does not seem to have been widespread. 'I too remember hearing about the forcible occupation of Hindu lands, and that some Hindu women were humiliated', the Assam official said. 'But I cannot give any specific instances based on firsthand information.' Likewise, another displaced Sylheti, Rathindranath Bhattacharjee from Dharmahat village, recalled, 'Because our district was in Assam at that time, our place was peaceful—there were no direct [communal] clashes there.'[69] As such, rumours appear to have played an important role in instigating fresh out-migration of Hindus from Sylhet, although in most cases such rumours were not borne out by facts. Several respondents spoke about one such incident they referred to as *Meghna nadir dangga*, the riot on the Meghna River, in 1950; there, they had heard of atrocities committed by Muslims on a train carrying Hindus to Dacca (later Dhaka).[70] One respondent based in Karimganj town also referred to this story, saying that he had heard that 'In Dacca, many Hindus were caught from the train . . . [They were] killed and thrown into the river. I heard that afterwards, as revenge, Muslims were attacked in Karimganj.'[71] Yet while some of the respondents did mention the 'tension', 'fear' or 'terror' that they experienced in the immediate aftermath of the Referendum, neither the Hindus nor Muslims could remember any major instance of violence in Sylhet, though there were cases of robberies, some houses were burned down, and stones were thrown at members of other communities. This is corroborated by Mojammil Ali Laskar of Cachar, in his autobiography.[72] The flow of events leading up to the Referendum and Partition of Sylhet that emerge from the eyewitness accounts highlights the multiple ways in which Partition of the Indian subcontinent unfolded in different parts of the region. The very fact that there was a referendum in Sylhet—ostenisbly to allow its people to influence their own destiny—makes its subsequent history different from that of Punjab or Bengal. While the considerably lower levels of physical violence further distinguished the experience of Sylhet, the inevitable flow of migrants across the borders, however, was not very different from the experience of its neighbour, Bengal, or the faraway

Punjab. In the final analysis, though the Sylhetis were more 'empowered' (by the fact of having had a referendum) than Punjab and Bengal whose people had to meekly accept the imperial vivisection of their homelands, they were no less victims of Partition in every sense of the word.

NOTES

1. Personal communication with eyewitness.
2. Ibid.
3. Ibid.
4. Ibid.
5. Digindra Chandra Datta, 'Aamar Atmakatha', in Nirmal Chandra Datta (ed.), *Adhyapak Digindra Chandra Datter Janma Shatabarshiki Swarani,* Kolkata: no publisher, 2000. (Translation from Bengali mine.)
6. Tanmay Bhattacharjee, *The Sylhet Referendum: A Study in Retrospect,* Silchar, 2006, pp. 232-3.
7. Ibid., p. 233.
8. *The Statesman*, 11 July 1947; *The Hindustan Times*, 11 July 1947.
9. Sanghamitra Pal Choudhury, 'Sylhet Referendum-1947', unpublished M.Phil. dissertation, North-Eastern Hill University, Shillong, 1992, p. 71.
10. Md. Gyasuddin.
11. Kayum Mia (b. 1932) in Patherkandi in Karimganj. His early political affiliation was to the Muslim League.
12. Abdus Shukkur Khan (b. 1932) in Sadarshi near the

current Bangladesh border. A resident of Karimganj, his early political affiliation was to the Jamiat Islam.

13. Abdul Latif (b. 1935) in Kanisail in Karimganj. His political affiliation was to the Muslim League.
14. Nazimuddin Ahmed (b. 1923) in Sylhet. His early education was in Sylhet. His early political affiliation was with the Communist Party.
15. Safik Ahmed (b. 1932) in Habiganj (later settled in Karimganj).
16. Abdullah Shakeel (b. 1930) in Karimganj town.
17. Moinuddin Choudhury (b. 1931) in Sharifnagar village in Karimganj. A resident of Karimganj, his early political affiliation was to the Jamiat Islam.
18. Abdullah Shakeel.
19. Badruddin Laskar (b. 1930) in Karimganj. Political affiliation was to the Muslim League.
20. Nazimuddin Ahmed (b. 1923) in Sylhet. His early education was in Sylhet. Early political affiliation was with the Communist Party.
21. Abdul Rashid (b. 1935) in Ratabari in Karimganj subdivision. He was not much politically minded and bore no affiliation to any political party at the time of the Referendum.
22. Ibid.
23. Rahman Mahmud Ansari (b. 1929), Badarpur, Sylhet.
24. Ibid.
25. Fazlul Hussain (DOB not available) but claims to have been about 25-30 years old in 1947.
26. Ibid.
27. Murakib Ali.
28. Abdul Noor.

29. Rahul Sheikh (b.1930) Sylhet town (now in Karimganj).
30. Ibid.
31. Abdul Matin (b. 1931), Deurail, Badarpur, Sylhet. Political affiliation with Jamiat.
32. Abdul Rashid (b. 1935).
33. Taibunissa.
34. Ibid.
35. Abdus Shukkur Khan.
36. Ibid.
37. Abdul Latif.
38. Ibid.
39. Taibunissa.
40. Tafajjul Ahmed (b. 1931) in Chandkhira in Karimganj. His political affiliation was to the Muslim League.
41. Abdul Noor (b. 1915). Village Maizbhi in Karimganj.
42. Abdul Matin.
43. Ibid.
44. Ibid.
45. Choudhuri, 1992, op. cit., p. 80.
46. Ibid., p. 81.
47. Abdul Noor.
48. Abdul Mannan.
49. Shafiqul Haque Chowdhury (b. 1933). Neelam-bazar, Karimganj.
50. Tafajjul Ahmed (b. 1931) Chandkhira, Karimganj.
51. Taibunissa.
52. Abdul Latif (b. 1934), Kanisail, Karimganj.
53. Ibid.
54. Murakib Ali.
55. Kayum Mia (b. 1932) Patherkandi, Karimganj.

56. Abdus Shukur Khan (10).
57. Abdul Jalil (b. 1932) Maizdhi, Karimganj.
58. Abdul Rashid.
59. Tafajjul Ahmed.
60. *Census of India 1951*, Report on Assam, p. xxxiii.
61. Ibid., p. xxxvi.
62. Ibid.
63. Ibid.
64. Ibid., p. 358.
65. Abdul Rashid.
66. Interviews with Partition eyewitnesses.
67. Ibid.
68. http://bhudevchakrabarty.rediffiland.com/blogs/2007/06/18/I-SING-THE-SONGS-OF-MY-SOUL-OF-THIS.html accessed on 17 July 2009.
69. Rathindra Nath Bhattacharjee interviewed in Tridib Chakrabarti, Nirupama Ray-Mandal and Paulami Ghosal (eds.), *Dhangsha O' Nirman: Bangiya Udbastu Samaj-er Swakathita Bibaran*, School of Cultural Texts and Records, Jadavpur University, 2007, p. 66.
70. Interviews with Partition eyewitnesses.
71. Born in 1932, the respondent belongs to Karimganj.
72. Laskar, pp. 131-2.

CHAPTER SIX

Partition and Migration

From the interviews discussed in the previous chapter, it appears that, for some years immediately following Partition, there was a relatively free and easy back-and-forth movement by people from both sides of the border. Interestingly, the Census of 1951 notes that groups of Hindu Sylhetis used to 'come and return to Sylhet still being unable to decide whether they should leave their home and hearth for good'.[1] It was only after the introduction of the passport system, in 1950, that this easy movement was checked. Either way, for many Sylhetis the 'real' Partition came only in 1950, after the terrible riots that took place in different parts of East Bengal, and with the imposition of a passport regime. Most people did not easily comprehend the real meaning of the partition of their ancestral land and country, and many had hoped that things would eventually go back to normal. Certainly, few imagined that lines drawn on maps would eventually lead to partitioned identities, memories and loyalties—the enormity of this new reality took several years to sink in.

In the end, however, the impact of the Referendum was different from what many had imagined. The general expectation that the separation of Sylhet would put an end to the Sylheti presence in Assam was to be proved wrong almost immediately, for Sylheti migrants began to enter Assam/India (including the residents of Karimganj which stayed with India) in large numbers from 1946 onwards.[2] The Assam Pradesh Congress had clearly miscalculated in the belief that Partition would get rid of both Sylhet and Sylhetis: the problem of the refugee influx (large sections of whom were Hindus from Sylhet) that was built into the emerging situation threatened to neutralize the gains achieved by the ouster of Sylhet.[3]

The Sylheti *bhadralok* who migrated permanently to India between 1946 and 1950 can be broadly divided into four groups, based on the time and conditions of migration. First, there were those who migrated from Sylhet to Assam for economic or familial reasons since its amalgamation with Assam long before 1947, but had continued to have a home in Sylhet. My grandfather, for instance, was one such who, as a police officer of the Assam government since 1923, was posted in different places in the region, including Manipur (under the Indian government until its formal integration with India in 1949-50), Dibrugarh, Gauhati, Sylhet town, Habiganj and Shillong. Such people lost their ancestral homes in 1947 when Sylhet was partitioned, but retained their new 'city' homes in other parts of Assam. Some others had left Sylhet in 1946 in fear for their lives, upon hearing news of communal atrocities in Noakhali, though their numbers were small. Around 150 of these uprooted families were rehabilitated in Assam; a refugee camp was set up opposite Cotton College in Gauhati, where the refugees were temporarily put up and later shifted to the Noakhali Colony in the Silpukhuri area of the city. By the end of 1946, as many as 6,860 individuals had migrated to India.[4] There was also some outmigration to Shillong by well-to-do Sylhetis soon after the news of the Referendum was announced. The 1951 *Census of India* explains the reasons why these people left Sylhet for Assam:

In Pakistan, the whole-scale opting out of experienced non-Muslim officers and their replacement by junior inexperienced Muslim officers greatly weakened the administrative machinery and created a general feeling of insecurity and lack of confidence in the bonafides of the new state.[5]

This, coupled with other facts, caused an exodus of Hindus from Pakistan to India.[6] These other elements particularly included the lessening of prospects for Hindus in government and administrative services; and in business and trade, which at the time depended largely on permits, licenses, and government sympathy and encouragement. In addition, there were examples of petty fanaticism and intolerant attitudes towards other religions, as well as the oft-repeated declarations of top-ranking Pakistani leaders that their new state would be purely Islamic, an ideology enshrined in the Objective Resolution of the Pakistan Constituent Assembly. Together, these inevitably created a situation that was hardly conducive to Hindus remaining in Pakistan, according to the 1951 census.

A second group of Sylheti *bhadralok* migrated almost immediately after the results of the Referendum were announced on 14 July. A fear of what might happen to them and their families prompted this group of people to leave Sylhet mostly during the period of 1947-9, and included the optees from both government and private enterprises (there were also small numbers of professionals and traders). The Assamese newspaper *Dainik Asamiya* reported on 20 August that large numbers of East Bengal migrants were entering Assam by rail at the time. Many lost their jobs, homes and property in East Bengal but followed the historical migration routes to Assam, where their extended families and friends had relocated during the colonial period and where they could, presumably, find safe haven. On 23 August, *Dainik Asamiya* reported that the Assam government had earlier sent out a circular to its employees in Sylhet district, offering them the option to choose which government they wished to serve after the Referendum, India or Pakistan. It also reported that the Assam government informed its employees that it was

> not bound in any way to keep them in respective employment for an indefinite time, and that also those who are employed temporarily in Assam government's job, cannot be promised by the government that they may become permanent one day.[7]

In August 1947 alone, as many as 12,297 persons migrated to Assam, followed by 6,348 in September and 4,409 in October. There was a further tailing-off thereafter, but the total never dipped below

2,000 in any month, save for November 1948 and October-November 1949.[8] One eyewitness from Sylhet (now living in the United States) migrated to Calcutta in January 1948 while he was studying at MC College in Sylhet. He recounted having to take his final examinations at Calcutta University as a 'non-collegiate refugee student'.[9] 'The Calcutta University was very kind and generous, and published an E.B. [East Bengal] application form to take the final exam technically as a non-collegiate displaced student from East Bengal', he said. 'Many [students] stayed back in Sylhet under Dacca University and moved to India later, and lost one or two years of their final studies in India.' He also recalled there were many other students in Sylhet who had lost the opportunity to take their final examinations under the Calcutta University (all Assam colleges were part of Calcutta University at that time) after Partition as it now fell on the other side of the border. He continued:

> Some Muslim students were devastated to lose their chance to take the supplemental examination under Calcutta university and they sought Baba's [his father, who was a professor of English] help. Baba [Father] made a trip to Calcutta on their behalf in October/November 1947 to plead with the Calcutta University authorities and obtained

permission for them to take the examination in Calcutta. All these unfortunate Muslim students accompanied me on train journey to Calcutta, some of them for the first time ever, in January 1948 and took the examinations.[10]

During this time, optees from both private enterprises and state and central government moved to India, and they were mostly Sylhetis.[11] For instance, there were several teachers from MC College in Sylhet who had opted to serve in Gauhati's prestigious Cotton College. Some of the optees, such as my grandfather who worked in the provincial police service, were reinstated; some others, however, were not, especially those employed in the higher-education sector. Some of the latter sued the state government, and several were indeed re-instated after lengthy civil suits.

In a booklet first published in 1950, K.B. Mukherjee (a pseudonym), one of the MC College teachers who had opted to go to India, explains the problems confronted by some optees after Partition. After the Assam government pulled out of Sylhet on 14 August 1947, several optees who had received transfer orders by that day were indeed successfully re-instated in Assam. But those who had not yet been served transfer orders, wrote Mukherjee, had a wholly different experience. On 13 August 1947, the Assam cabinet decided that any government servant who was a native of or domiciled in Sylhet district, and had been posted there as of 14 August 1947, should remain there irrespective of his choice of where to serve, and should not be exchanged with an officer outside Sylhet who may have opted to go to Pakistan. The statement further stated that the Assamese government would take no further responsibility for such officers who stayed back after 15 August. Mukherjee writes that about 1,496 employees of the Assamese government, including 422 temporary employees, were ultimately left behind in Sylhet due to this decision.

On the side of the government, it was stated that against 1,729 employees of Assam who opted for Pakistan, 1,496 employees in Sylhet had opted for India. Of the latter, 1,153 (more than 75 per cent) were placed in employment by July 1948, leaving a balance of 353 individuals yet to be absorbed. The main reason for not taking in all Sylhet employees in vacancies created by employees who opted for Pakistan was that total cadres were reduced by about 25 per cent due to Sylhet's secession from Assam.[12] Mukherjee himself had to fight a long civil suit against the state government, only to be offered a five-year contract as the head of the Department of English at Cotton College from 1952-7.[13]

In 1947-8, the largest single number of optees was made up of employees of a private enterprise called Assam Railways,[14] which had its original headquarters in Chittagong. After Partition, the railway workshop was split into three parts and shifted to Dibrugarh-Naliyapul, Pandu and Gauhati. Settlement areas or 'colonies' were started next to the Noakhali Colony in Silpukhuri for these optees, which the general-secretary of the All Assam Refugee Association at that time, Bijoy Kumar Das, numbered at about 7,000. Inevitably, there were significant political ramifications to such large-scale influx. In particular, the migration of large groups of Sylheti migrants gave a boost to the nascent Communist Party in Assam, which was able to draw support from these migrants and open new bases in Gauhati, Pandu and Naliyapul areas. Demonstrations were organized regularly in these areas, as well as in Mariani near Dibrugarh.[15] Das recalls that some of the optees came to Assam 'like tourists, camera in hand . . . as if on a holiday', and in their wake came large numbers of relatives and friends.

My grandfather's home in Shillong was filled with such refugees (from Sylhet) between 1947 and 1949. In fact, when he returned from a brief posting in Manipur, he had to rent a small house for himself, as his own was too full. He assisted some of these individuals in finding jobs in the Police Wireless Organization, and by 1950 most of the houseguests had found their ways out of our family home.

The third group of *bhadralok* and other migrants was those who moved in large numbers to Assam and parts of Bengal in the immediate aftermath of the 1950 East Bengal riots. The main refugee influx to Assam took place during the three months from February to April 1950, following instances of violence elsewhere in East Pakistan; at one point, their number must have exceeded 500,000.[16] The April Agreement between the prime ministers of India and Pakistan brought back a sense of security among these terror-stricken masses, as a result of which large numbers returned to Pakistan—some 274,455 in all, as revealed by the census.[17] Of these, 144,512, or slightly more than half of the East Bengali refugees in Assam, came during 1950,[18] and almost all were from Sylhet. As such, the largest number of these refugees (93,177) was sheltered in Cachar district, due to its proximity to Sylhet.[19] Importantly, there had been no system of registration of displaced persons until the arrival of these 'new' refugees in 1950.[20] Even after the formal registration process began, the last date of such registration was 31 July 1951,[21] and the displaced persons who entered north-east India after that date were therefore not enumerated.

The fourth group of Sylheti 'migrants' were those who had homes in the four *thanas* of Ratabari, Patherkandi, Karimganj and Badarpur, and thus became Indians by dint of the land on which they lived when the Partition lines were drawn. They became Indian citizens without having to move anywhere; nor did they lose any property in those areas, though some did lose jobs or businesses on the East Pakistan side.

Some critical differences between Hindu and Muslim Sylheti Partition migration were (i) the numbers of Muslim migrants to India were considerably less than the Hindus, (iii) for Muslims both from the retained parts of Sylhet and other areas of Assam, it was more a decision 'to stay' whereas the Hindus of Sylhet had to make the decision 'to go'. The Hindu families in the three retained *thanas*, of course, were exceptions to this because they too, like the Muslims had the option to stay back in their ancestral homes, and (iii) there were several cases of Muslim Sylhetis initially moving to East Pakistan, and shortly afterwards returning to Assam to claim their original homes and lands.

A large number of Muslims migrated out of Assam to different parts of East Bengal after the 1950 riots. Many Bodos and Bengali Hindus from Kokrajhar area, near the Bongaigaon railway station (close to Assam's western border with East Pakistan), settled on lands left behind by these Muslims. The *Census of India* for 1951 puts the total number of Muslim emigrants from Assam to East Bengal at the time as 100,000.[22] According to the Nehru-Liaquat Pact of 1950 (signed to alleviate the fears of minorities and re-establish an environment of communal peace), all such lands were declared 'evacuee property', which would have to be returned to the original owners should they return within the next five years, a responsibility taken on by the governments themselves. But meanwhile it was decided to allot such land to local farmers who would be recognized as 'allottees' for the interim period. Each allottee would have to pay Rs. 10 per *bigha* (a variable measurement of land area) as revenue. In fact, when Muslims arrived in East Pakistan, they often informally exchanged land with local Hindus who were moving out to Assam. But such exchanges were not legal, given that all such lands were now under the government's prerogative as 'allotted' properties. In such cases, when some Muslims returned before the lapse of the mandatory five years, considerable tensions arose between the evacuee and the original owner. There were also instances in which Muslim men took their sons with them and went to East Pakistan, leaving the women at home in India.

At the height of the refugee flow, Assam hosted as few as 28 refugee camps sheltering about 8,000 displaced persons. At first, most of these camps came into being through the efforts of non-official bodies, though within a few weeks they were taken over by the state government.[23] By 1 January 1951, the number was down to seven camps, accommodating about 3,500 individuals. The last camp was closed by the end of September 1951.

Overall, far more people settled in the plain areas of Assam than in the hills. The district that sheltered the largest numbers of migrants was Cachar, due to its proximity to Sylhet, while the next largest settlements were in Goalpara, Kamrup,

Nowgong, Darrang, Sibasagar and Lakhimpur in Assam. In the Hills Division, most refugees settled in the United Khasi and Jaintia Hills, followed by the Garo Hills, the United Mikir and North Cachar Hills. As noted, there are no available figures on the unofficial migrants, but on the basis of field visits and interviews it can be safely said that the figures of those who came unofficially far outstripped that of those that came officially. The *Census of 1951*, which was the first ever to be taken in independent India, contains a special section on the Partition-displaced population in its report on Assam. However R.G. Vaghaiwalla, the census commissioner, himself points out the challenges of preparing the census so soon after Partition. The huge problems of the relief and rehabilitation of large numbers of Partition migrants necessitated the formulation of a special question regarding 'refugees' in this census, at the request of the Central Ministry of Rehabilitation.

It is also possible to compare the findings of the refugee census of 1949 with the *Census of 1951*, to look for discrepancies. Vaghaiwalla himself points out that in the case of Cachar, for instance, the total number of displaced persons in 1951 (93,177) appears to be under-enumerated when compared with the numbers in 1949 (55,000), especially when one remembers that there was a 'tremendous influx of refugees especially in the early months of 1950'.[24] On the other hand, he also notes that many individuals who had already been settled in Cachar either in service, business or trade tried to be counted as refugees. The usual plea was either that, though they had long settled in Cachar, following Partition they no longer had any control over their properties in Pakistan; or that it was only after Partition that they made up their minds to settle for good in India.[25] Many refugees, on the other hand, registered as indigenous persons of Assam at the time of the enumeration, in view of the government policy of according primacy to such individuals in employment, allotment of government lands and distribution of permits, licenses and contracts.[26] Gathering correct information was made still more difficult by the constant movement of the displaced from one location to another. Moreover, a number of Sylhetis were noted to have been moving back and forth between Sylhet and Assam even after Partition, and it is possible that many were absent during the enumeration. Finally, a large number of 'needy people' from the East Pakistan side were also seen to have crossed borders temporarily, in order to avail of relief measures.

THE MEANINGS OF PARTITION: MUSLIM AND HINDU SYLHETIS

Looking back more than a half-century later, what did the Referendum and Partition mean to the Sylhetis? Nizamuddin Ahmed's eyes turned misty when this question was put to him. He had a long history of political participation behind him—despite being a staunch believer in Communist ideology, he had even joined the Swadeshi and Salt Satyagraha calls of Mahatma Gandhi, and had served jail time. As he tried to look back and remember details of the Referendum and Partition, he grew visibly saddened, saying, *Sylhet partitioner katha koiya labh nai!* (There is no point in talking about the Sylhet Partition anymore). Partition became such a cause of grief for many that 'people could not feel the joy of independence,' said Mohammed Gyasuddin.[27] In many families, brothers were now separated—one living in East Pakistan and the other in India. Before Partition, too, people lived in different places, 'but it was not a problem as people did not feel like they were living miles apart, as they did now', Gyasuddin said. Partition has shattered 'the emotional bonding among people'.[28]

Nazimuddin Ahmed himself used to regularly travel from his home in Sylhet town to the one in Karimganj. *Sylheti-r madhye jhagra lagia bhinna matir shristi hoise* (Now due to quarrels among Sylhetis themselves, the land has been separated), he said. There is now little communication with relatives who found themselves living in East Pakistan, now Bangladesh, after Partition. Had there been no Partition, he believed that life would have been better for both communities. However, if Partition had to happen, in his opinion it would have been better for Sylhet to have stayed in India, while the Barak Valley region (Cachar) could have gone to East Pakistan.

Abdul Mannan grew visibly agitated, at times angry, when he spoke of Partition. To explain the Partition experience, he narrated the story of three brothers living in Sylhet district before Partition. They used to have 2 *bighas* of land, but after Partition one and a half *bigha* fell in East Pakistan. Due to the political circumstances of the time, two brothers were forced to settle on the Pakistan side of the land, while one stayed back in India. Their economic conditions deteriorated as the size of their agricultural land shrunk, and the family ties also became weakened. 'They aspired to live together some day, but their voices were not heard', he said. 'Thus, Partition has caused not only physical demarcation but also a line that has destroyed the simple and smooth lives of many people.'[29]

S.R. Laskar, from Patherkandi, was short of hearing and had to be helped by his children to tell his story from that era. But he was still very articulate. *Gano vote jibanta sesh karia dilo* (The Referendum has ruined our lives), he said.[30] Two of his brothers went to East Pakistan and started a business there. In the beginning they used to come back once a year for a visit, but that slowly stopped. Now, both are dead, and Laskar was pained to say that his family had no connection with his brother's children. 'All those things happened only due to Partition—the Partition of Sylhet was not at all good', he said.[31] Laskar believed that it would have been 'far better' if Patharkandi and other areas (such as Ratabari) had gone to Pakistan instead: 'There are lots of mosques in East Pakistan and Muslims could have had a better life there.'[32] Laskar said that he himself had wanted to leave for Pakistan, but his father refused, as they had significant agricultural lands on the Indian side. Such a move would not have made economic sense for the family, and so they stayed back. The same happened with Abdus Shukkur Khan's family, whose members remained in India as they were dependent on agriculture, and his father anticipated that their agricultural livelihood might not prosper in Pakistan.[33]

As noted earlier, there were also instances of Muslims initially migrating to Pakistan and then reversing the decision soon afterwards and returning to India. For instance, Moshaid Ali said that at the time of Partition many Muslims were unhappy because they were numerically and politically weak; East Pakistan being a Muslim-majority state thus held a natural attraction for them. Many people, including Ali, subsequently began to exchange their property with Hindus in Pakistan, often through common acquaintances. One of his brothers went to Pakistan on the basis of such an understanding, so he too decided to do the same—going with his three sons while keeping his wife and daughters at his home in Patherkandi. He had almost fixed a land exchange with a Hindu counterpart in East Pakistan; but after staying for a few months he desperately wanted to return to his home in India. For him, in the final analysis, a 'place of birth is something more worthy than that of religious and other sentiments'.[34] Had there been no Partition, he said, people would have led 'better, happier and more-contented lives'.[35]

After Partition Murakib Ali's family also exchanged land with a Hindu, and moved to the Kashinagar area near Sylhet. But after a few months, the Hindu family had shifted to another place. Murakib Ali's family now decided to return to Karimganj for economic reasons. *Pakistan-e gelam, kintu krishi karbar nai, kita karia khaitai? Gatike abar amra aigelam and dekhlam anya kutumra bara khushi karla amrare paiya* (We went to Pakistan, but we couldn't do agriculture over there—how do we eat then? So, we came back again and found that our relatives were very happy to have us back), he said.[36] Kayum Mia's family too had decided to move to Pakistan in the wake of the post-Partition communal tensions, ending up in a place called Juri in Sylhet, where they lived like refugees for a while, all together in a large house. Eventually finding such living arrangements difficult they came back to Karimganj, only to find that a Hindu family had moved into their ancestral home. After many requests, the new residents agreed to spare a single room for Kayum Mia's family; only after the intervention of a Hindu manager of the local Motor Association was the Hindu family eventually settled elsewhere.

The resolution to that particular situation notwithstanding, this dynamic generally has been repeatedly flagged as a significant and ongoing problem. 'Refugees coming from East Pakistan have not been properly settled, which is creating problems in the Hindu-Muslim relations in Assam today', said Murakib Ali.[37] Some eyewitnesses specifically pointed to the infamous Nellie Massacre of 1980—in which a large number of Muslims of East Bengal origin were killed by local tribal communities—as being a significant dark spot in the history of Muslims in Assam who had chosen to remain in India in 1947.[38] 'Before Partition, labourers were brought [to Assam] from East Bengal to till the soil. But now these people are looked down upon', said Abdul Mannan.[39]

Ultimately, of course, Partition created identity problems for both Sylheti Hindus and Muslims in India, by reducing their numbers and turning them into small minorities. If Partition was at all required, 'the whole Bengali-dominated regions should have been transferred to East Pakistan, keeping the community intact,' said Mannan.[40] While the Sylheti people today are scattered all over India, Shafiqul Haq Choudhury said that they were getting their due recognition only in the Barak Valley.[41] Abdul Jalil was highly emotional when he said, *Ganovote ta hoilo manusher ichcha janar lagia, kintu manushe to janlo na kene amrare alga kara hoilo* (The Referendum was organized to know the people's wishes, but the people never got to know why they were separated).

It is an irony that even after the separation of Sylhet, Assam (and north-east India generally) remained thickly populated by persons of Sylheti origin, both Hindus and Muslims. The reasons for this are not hard to uncover. A shared history with the people of Assam—with all its colonial linkages, both economic and social—were among the primary reasons why many first-generation Sylheti Hindus preferred to settle in this region after Partition. 'These were all familiar places for us', explained one Sylheti *bhadralok* settler in Assam.

> From our childhood we have been visiting Shillong to meet my uncles, and Gauhati to meet my maternal grandparents.

From Ward's Lake [in Shillong] to the Kamakhya Hills [in Gauhati], we knew almost every nook and corner. This was not a new country for us.[42]

Besides, as mentioned earlier, those Hindus and Muslims whose land, properties and jobs were in the retained part also chose to remain in their original homelands. The small group of optees as well exercised their option to settle on the Indian side.

As for the emotional cost of Partition, the Hindus responded pretty much the same way as their Muslim counterparts. There was the same regret, the same sorrow and pain, but the rationale was different. Hindus suffered less from broken families as they left in entire families whenever possible or in phases otherwise. During the interviews we rarely came across instances where Hindu siblings or families were separated due to Partition. The fact that the *bhadralok* were more affluent, a stronger social network in Assam and that they had simultaneous homes in the two valleys helped them to move in entire families. While the Muslims felt that all of Sylhet should have been ceded to East Pakistan, the Hindus naturally felt that Sylhet should not have been partitioned in the first place.

The areas that had a large Sylheti population before 1947 also became the favourite relocation spots for new Hindu settlers, who once again remained concentrated in urban areas and crowded into the professions, as before. Several 'refugee' pockets emerged in Assam and the surrounding region, such as Shillong and Tura (now in Meghalaya), the Cachar Valley, the erstwhile princely state of Tripura and in some of the urban localities of the Brahmaputra Valley. From the 1951 census details, it appears that such populations were most pronounced in the towns of Shillong, Silchar, Nowgong, Gauhati, Dibrugarh, Lumding and Karimganj, the same places that possessed a sizeable Sylheti population in the days before Partition.

The preference of the Sylheti *bhadralok* to settle in urban areas or city outskirts was because these areas were most likely to provide 'miscellaneous' sources of employment and also because these were the areas where their extended kin were also settled. It is important to note, however, that very few Sylheti *bhadraloks* were actual liabilities for the state, and that their histories of relocation were different from their Muslim counterparts. By the early 1960s, most had managed to establish themselves comfortably in and around Assam.[43] On being asked whether he had taken help from the government in rehabilitating himself in India after migration, Rathindranath Bhattacharjee from Sylhet, responded, 'I managed to stay with my relatives. They also helped me to get a job, so I did not have to go to the government for help'[44] (translation from Bengali mine). As to why the Sylheti *bhadralok* were able to relocate in post-colonial Assam without financial assistance from the government, respondents principally cited familiarity with Assam, educational qualification, and support from relatives already living in Assam.

Ultimately, it becomes clear that the Sylheti *bhadralok's* experience of the 1947 Partition was quite different from many of the other groups of Partition migrants whose experiences have thus far been studied. No doubt international migration anywhere in the world has generally been easier for educated middle-class migrants or professionals; but it must be remembered that Partition migration was no ordinary migration. Rather, it was the culmination of communal rivalry and antagonism that overtook subcontinental politics and society starting in the early 1940s, and much of the population displacement that followed was involuntary and at the risk of life and property. Large sections of the middle classes and professionals in the Punjab and some parts of Bengal (both Hindus and Muslims) equally bore the brunt of communal violence and pauperization, along with their less fortunate counterparts, and faced enormous difficulties following post-Partition migration to India or Pakistan.[45] In Sylhet, however, the middle classes did not encounter such a high scale of violence or destitution at the time of Partition, or even immediately afterwards, particularly in the 1947-50 period that this study is focused on. However, this did not necessarily lessen the trauma associated with leaving behind one's homeland, nor was the relocation process easy in emotional, familial, social or even economic terms. There were, of course, cases like that of my father's cousin in Guwahati, Subir Jethu, who had faced the very worst of Partition because he did not possess the crucial Sylheti *bhadralok* characteristic-education.

I have discussed elsewhere that the nostalgia of the lost homeland in Sylhet still persists among first-generation Sylhetis, and sometimes atavistically among some younger India-born Sylhetis as well.[46] Sixty years afterwards, when asked *Desh kothaye?* (Where is your country/home?), many would almost involuntarily answer, 'Sylhet'. In another context, Frank H. Wu has explored (in an article titled 'Where Are You Really From? Asian Americans and the Perpetual Foreigner Syndrome') the difference in perception of being 'from' somewhere and 'really from' somewhere.

> 'Where are you from?' is a question I like answering.
>
> 'Where are you really from?' is a question I really hate answering.
>
> 'Where are you from?' is a question we all routinely ask one another upon meeting a new person.
>
> 'Where are you really from?' is a question some of us tend to ask others of us very selectively.
>
> For Asian Americans, the questions frequently come paired like that. Among ourselves, we can even joke nervously about how they just about define the Asian American experience. More than anything else that unifies us, everyone with an Asian face who lives in America is afflicted by the perpetual foreigner syndrome. We are figuratively and even literally returned to Asia and ejected from America.[47]

The Sylheti Partition migration experience is caught in a similar existential dilemma. It has been further intensified by the growing politicization of post-colonial nativist narratives in north-east India, which have often constructed Partition-era migrants, along with other immigrant groups, as *bohiragoto*, or outsiders. Historian Sujit Chaudhuri writes that the Referendum-driven separation of Sylhet had its origin in what can be termed a long-cherished quest by the natives of Assam, that of carving out a homogeneous province for themselves.

The Assamese, he writes, perceived Partition as a 'God-sent opportunity' to attain that role, as Sylhet was seen as 'an ulcer hindering the emergence of a unilingual Assam'.[48] Even after Independence and Partition, the tenor of local politics was coloured by powerful strands of inter-community competition, much of which was rooted in the original decision, by the East India Company administrators in 1874, to attach Bengali-speaking Sylhet to Assam. It was thus a coincidence that this decision also divided the community along Hindu-Muslim lines. On the other hand, the Sylhetis themselves have kept alive a duality in their cultural identity, the result of a struggle to remember and retain their essential 'Sylheti-ness'. While in the midst of acculturating within the larger Assamese identity, one part of the Sylheti mind still carries nostalgia for a lost homeland that many Sylhetis have never actually seen

—an imagined loyalty to an imagined homeland that is also related to their minority status within the post-colonial state of Assam.

NOTES

1. *Census of India* 1951, vol. XII, Assam, Manipur and Tripura, Government of India, p. 358.
2. Sujit Chaudhuri, 'A God-sent Opportunity', www.india-seminar.com/2002/510/510%20chaudhuri.htm, 2002, retrieved on 5 November 2007.
3. Ibid.
4. *Census of India* 1951, p. 359.
5. Ibid., p. 356.
6. Ibid.
7. All the reports published in *Dainik Asamiya* were translated into English by Khaleda Sultana for this research project.
8. *Census of India* 1951, op. cit., p. 359.
9. Personal communication with author.
10. Mihir Chandra Datta, 'The Patriarch as I Remember Him', in Nihar Ranjan Datta and Mihir Kanti Datta (eds), *Adhyapak Digindra Chandra Datta-r Janma Satabarshiki Swarani*, Kolkata, p. 126.
11. About 1,800 officers of Sylhet district opted to serve India instead of Pakistan after the Referendum. They did so on unequivocal terms, guaranteed by that government regarding uninterrupted retention of their existing terms and conditions of service including seniority. But when, after Partition, they were discharged by the Government

of Pakistan, newly established in Sylhet, the Government of Assam transferred from Sylhet to the rest of Assam every Assamese save a small proportion of others; and a vast number was either discharged on gratuity or premature pension, or kept on a temporary basis as juniors to their own former juniors, see J.K. Chowdhury, op. cit., 1954.

12. Mukherjee, op.cit.
13. Ibid., p. 47.
14. Conversations with Bijoy Kumar Das, General-Secretary of All Assam Refugee Association, Guwahati.
15. All information regarding employees of Assam Railways are collected from a series of interviews with Bijoy Kumar Das.
16. *Census of India 1951*, p. 357.
17. Ibid.
18. Ibid.
19. Ibid.
20. Ibid., p. 360.
21. Ibid.
22. Monirul Hussain, *The Assam Movement: Class, Ideology, Identity*, New Delhi: Manak Publication, 1993, p. 210.
23. *Census of India 1951*, p. 360.
24. Ibid., p. 357.
25. Ibid.
26. Ibid., p. 358.
27. Md. Gyasuddin.
28. Ibid.
29. Abdul Mannan.
30. S.R. Laskar, Patherkandi.
31. Ibid.

32. Laskar.
33. Abdus Shukkur Khan.
34. Moshaid Ali, n.d, Patherkandi.
35. Ibid.
36. Murakib Ali.
37. Ibid.
38. Abdul Mannan, Hailakandi.
39. Ibid.
40. Abdul Mannan.
41. Shafiqul Haq Choudhury.
42. Interview with eyewitness.
43. Monirul Hussain, 'Refugees in the Face of Emerging Ethnicity in North East India: An overview', *Studies in Humanities and Social Sciences*, 2(1) 1995, p. 123.
44. Rathindra Nath Bhattacharjee a Sylheti interviewed in Tridib Chakrabarti, Nirupama Ray-Mandal and Paulami Ghosal (eds.), *Dhangsha O'Nirman: Bangiya Udbastu Samaj-er Swakathita Bibaran*, school of Cultural Texts and Records, Jadavpur University, 2007, p. 66.
45. Ishtiaq Ahmed, 'Forced Migration and Ethnic Cleansing in Lahore in 1947: Some first-person accounts', www.sacw.net/partition/june2004Ishtiaq Ahmed.pdf (2004), accessed on 24 June 2006.
46. Anindita Dasgupta, 'Remembering Sylhet: A Forgotten Story of India's 1947 Partition', *Economic and Political Weekly,* 43(31)2008.
47. http://findarticles.com/p/articles/mi_m0HSP/is_1_6/ai_106647778/, accessed on 14 October 2007.
48. Chaudhuri, 2002, op. cit.

CHAPTER SEVEN

Conclusion

The inclusion of Sylhet—and the English-educated Sylhetis—into Assam in 1874 remained controversial throughout much of the nineteenth and twentieth century. However, by the 1930s both the Assamese and Sylhetis had come to accept it as a fait accompli, and learnt to live with it even if grudgingly. As has been discussed earlier in the book, two other closely related developments complicated the issue of Sylhet in Assam: the first was the large-scale migration of the Mymensinghiyas and the subsequent increase in the number of Muslims in Assam; and second, the demand made by the Muslim League that Assam, due to its large Muslim population, be included into Jinnah's proposed six-province Pakistan. It was only then that the old faultlines of Assamese politics—regulation of peasant migration from East Bengal, and the separation of Sylhet—resurfaced in a different garb in the 1940s. What was essentially rooted in a 'valley-jealousy' and competition over land now re-invented itself with the onset of communal politics.

The narratives of Sylheti eyewitnesses of the Referendum and Partition help to recreate the story from a people's perspective, and some interesting conclusions emerge from their testimonies. It seems quite clear that Sylheti Hindus and Muslims remembered the Referendum and Partition differently and eclectically at the time they were interviewed. In other words, each community decided what it wanted to remember and re-tell, and what to forget. For instance, even 60-odd years afterwards, in the Sylheti Hindu discourse, the feelings of loss, fear, sadness and a resignation to fate persisted along with a sense of having been abandoned by all in 1947. In these accounts, the Sylheti Hindu was constructed as a lone fighter, braving all the odds against himself on the two fateful days of the Referendum, and marching ahead only to face the inevitable defeat in the end. Even the monsoon rains seemed to have conspired with the political leaders, district administration and British government to deliver an unbearable electoral loss to this Sylheti Braveheart! A class element also crept into this analysis when some Hindus felt that the Referendum provided the socio-economically backward Sylheti Muslims an opportunity to strike back at the upper- and middle-class Sylheti *bhadralok* dominance. It is equally significant that unlike professional historians, the Sylheti Hindu respondents saw the Referendum primarily as a result of communal politics, not of language. Again, most Sylheti Hindu saw the loss of their homeland as being inevitable after the Referendum results were announced, as if an invisible hand had pushed them out of their ancestral homes. Finally, the Sylheti *bhadralok* narratives also emphasize, perhaps to minimize/deny the impact of Partition on their lives, that none of them had been pauperized or faced violence in the course of Referendum and Partition.

As argued before, several factors made it possible for the Sylheti *bhadralok* to relocate in Assam without experiencing direct violence or pauperization. I will outline here five of the most critical ones. First, the Sylheti *bhadralok* had a long history of migration into parts of the colonial province of Assam, of which Sylhet was a part from 1874 until 1947. The lives of many upper- and middle-class Sylhetis, including my grandfather, straddled both the Assam and Surma Valleys as early as the turn of the century, as they were employed in the colonial bureaucracy and other sectors of the province's economy. As such, when Partition took place many of them were already living and working in Assam, while several others owned land and property in both the Brahmaputra and Barak valleys. Thus, the Sylheti *bhadralok* studied in this book had all the benefits of social networks as second- or third-generation migrants in Assam.

Second, the Sylheti *bhadralok* had long-established social networks in those areas of Assam to which they relocated following Partition, even in cases in which their lives and livelihoods had not straddled the two valleys.[1] Third, neither Sylhet nor Assam experienced the scale of actual violence that was faced by communities in Punjab and Bengal during the period of 1946-50. Of course, this is not to suggest that Sylhet and Assam were free from communal tension or instances of criminal activities at that time. Fourth, as a class, the Sylheti *bhadralok* were English-educated, and even those who were not optees found it comparatively easier to find livelihoods in Assam or in other parts of India, even abroad. And fifth, according to the Cyril Radcliffe's final drawings, three-and-a-half *thanas* of Sylhet (Patherkandi, Ratabari, Karimganj and Badarpur) were retained in Assam; the Sylhetis living here became Indians without having to move anywhere, and without losing any property in these areas. Though some of them did leave behind jobs on the other side (East Pakistan) of the border, and some businesses were affected for the same reason, the impact of Partition was still less harsh on this population when compared to their counterparts in Bengal or the Punjab.

Such a construction of *bhadralok* migrants might be different from the more familiar images that have come to dominate popular perceptions over the years. For instance, one unifying theme in the recent surge of 'new' Partition histories has been a desire to resurrect the experience of Partition migrants by recounting the violence that 'surrounded, accompanied and constituted' Partition.[2] Historians have also written powerful ethnographies that recapture the 'tremendous human cost, the dispossession and anguish of millions, and the violence and brutalities'[3] and the haunting memories of 'the smell of burning flesh, and screams of the victims of the 1947 riots'.[4] Violence, flight and suffering against a backdrop of communal violence and terror are central to this academic—as well as popular—

construction of Partition migrants. Set against such imagery, the experience of the Sylheti *bhadralok* is particularly important to understand the multiplicity of Partition experiences.

On the other hand, the Sylheti Muslims interviewed for this book did not have as easy a transition into independent India as did the Sylheti Hindu *bhadralok*. This is partly because many of the Muslim population in the Karimganj area were agriculturalists, and their decision to move or stay was determined by which side of the border their lands had fallen after Partition. Just like the Hindus, there was considerable back-and-forth movement among the Sylheti Muslims, especially in the period 1947-50. What was different about the Muslim narratives, however, was the air of expectation and excitement that surrounded the entire community on the eve and during the Referendum: the hope that the Referendum would be the first step toward achieving the much-cherished goal of joining a Muslim-majority country, Pakistan. Instead, in the Hindu narratives, there is a sense of desolation that ran through the entire period of Referendum and Partition, with Hindu voices considerably subdued right from the time the announcement was made. The Hindus and the Jamiat interviewees considered the referendum as a loss; many of the Muslims on the other hand, took it as an opportunity. The supporters of the Muslim League were overjoyed when the result was announced, only to be followed by a great sense of confusion—and ultimately, betrayal—when it was again announced two days later that the four *thanas* of Patherkandi, Karimganj, Badarpur and Ratabari had been conceded to India. For the Hindus and the Jamiat supporters, however, who were devastated by the results (though it was not entirely unexpected), were somewhat assuaged by this decision two days afterwards. That aside, both communities looked back at the July Referendum and Partition with a sense of sorrow and regret: by and large, for the Muslims it was a missed opportunity and for the Hindus it was a betrayal.

The testimonies also brought forth the tensions between the supporters of the Jamiat and the Muslim League, both of which were Muslims. This difference became sharper during the two or three days during which it was mistakenly announced that the whole of Sylhet (including Karimganj) had fallen to Pakistan, and heightened the social dilemma of the Jamiat supporters who were being seen as 'traitors' by the pro-League Muslims. It is interesting that some Jamiat supporters felt that their condition during those few days was actually worse than that of the Hindus, whose pro-India position could be justified on grounds of their religion. But what is strikingly clear from the narratives of both Hindus and Muslims is that, at least in the period 1947-50, there were no major instances of communal violence in Sylhet. This leads me to suggest that some of the Partition migration in these immediate years took place without actual acts of physical violence. However, I do not rule out the suggestion that though there was no 'actual' physical violence, much of the migration was precipitated by a fear or apprehension arising out of rumours and lack of understanding of political processes (such as the Referendum and Partition) by ordinary peoples.This is in itself a puzzle because in Sylhet, the result of the Referendum was seen as the direct handiwork of Sylheti people themselves, and when Partition came, it too was seen to have correctly reflected 'people's wishes'. Thus, each individual as it were, was held responsible for the final outcome of the referendum. In the communally charged situation in Sylhet, and the rest of India, at that time it would have been no surprise if there had been violence (like in Punjab and Bengal) between communities due to the way they had—or not—voted during or soon after Partition.

From the narratives above, it seems that land and livelihood were major factors in influencing the Muslim decision to migrate. To that extent, one might say that even after casting a vote in favour of one or the other country, the Muslim farmers had to wait for the final decision made by the Boundary Commission to decide where exactly the Partition lines would fall. In other words, a supporter of the Muslim League might have voted for Pakistan, but might have reluctantly decided to remain in India because his land and properties fell on the Indian side of the border. This gave rise to a feeling of having been cheated in spite of having scrupulously exercised their right to vote. What was incomprehensible to many then, was the whole point of the exercise in the first place, which in the aftermath struck some as having been pointless. The objective of the Referendum was to allow the people to decide for themselves where they wanted to live after Partition; but for many Muslims, when they learnt their lands had fallen on the Indian side, to them it seemed that their vote had been betrayed. Thus neither the Hindus, nor a section of Muslims, felt that the Referendum had served its stated purpose. Again, now that some of them had little choice but to stay back on the Indian side, they felt that they had become hostages of sorts as their loyalty became questionable due to the way they had voted in the Referendum.

The Muslims of Karimganj also had to deal with the issue of broken families. There were instances where some family members had voluntarily decided to go to Pakistan while some had to stay back despite having voted to go to Pakistan. Partition had also created a new minority, the Sylheti Muslim, in Assam after Partition. In fact, as a minority, this religious community had faced a whole range of issues in post-colonial Assam, which they felt were more challenging than the Partition problems because their identity was often mixed up with that of post-1971 undocumented immigrants from Bangladesh—with whom they shared a common ethnicity and religion—an unresolved political problem (until today) in post-colonial Assam. All in all, the Sylheti Muslims interviewed in Assam felt that Partition had not been good in hindsight because of (i) fragmented lands and families, (ii) because the whole of Sylhet did not go to East Pakistan in spite of the July Referendum results, (iii) the post-colonial minoritization of Bengali-speaking Muslims, and (iv) the socio-economic conditions of Muslims in post-colonial Assam.

In the end, however, the Indian Sylheti experience of the Referendum and Partition appears to have been problematic for both Hindus and Muslims. Today, a sense of victimization still runs through this entire community, regardless of religious affiliation, which was 'minoritized' following the fragmentation of the Sylheti identity into two, Indian and East Pakistani (later Bangladeshi). Both the Muslims and Hindus of Sylhet were affected by the decision to partition the district, though in different ways.

What made Sylhet's case particularly different from the Punjab or Bengal is its unique history of being separated from East Bengal and attached to Assam for 70 years, despite protests from Assamese and Sylhetis alike. This, after all, was what created the powerful local context for Partition. The idea of the Referendum may have been the result of the national context, or of Assam's inclusion in Jinnah's six-province vision of Pakistan. However, it was the local context that told much of the real story—and explained the lack of a major outcry against its partition, as it culled away most parts of a district that was unwelcome in Assam in the first place. Thus, even six decades later, the story of Sylhet continues to remain caught within the acutely personal realms of the Sylheti memory, nostalgia and imagination and living-room conversations.

Until newer research is carried out, the memory of an imagined homeland will continue to beckon the Indian Sylhetis into the corridors of history. Just like a young Sylheti, Nirmalya Chaudhury, based in Europe, wrote to me that 'the most coveted asset' of his family 'was a tattered black-and-white photograph and a letter' that was usually read out in every family gathering. The letter was from a relative who lives in Dhaka, and describes his excitement when he recently visited Sylhet 'his birthplace, our place'. The photograph was a picture of a broken-down temple that, Chaudhury said, 'was on our land built by our ancestors'. The joy he would see on the face of his (Indian) family members while the letter was read out, he said, 'showed how the Sylhetis even today crave for their [lost] land'.[5]

NOTES

1. For instance, my father recalls that their home was crowded with relatives, some of them distantly related, from Sylhet soon after my grandfather took up his new position in Shillong. Some of the younger boys from Sylhet, he recalls,` stayed with him for several years, after which they slowly started moving out.
2. Gyanendra Pandey, 'The Prose of Otherness', in David Arnold and David Hardiman (eds.), *Subaltern Studies*, vol. VIII, Delhi: Oxford, 1994, p. 5.
3. Mushirul Hassan, *Legacy of a Divided Nation: India's Muslims since Independence*, Boulder: Westview Press, 1997.
4. Ali, quoted in Ishtiaq Ahmed, 'The Lahore Effect', *Seminar*, www.india-seminar.com/2006/567/567_ishtiaq_ahmed.htm retrieved on 4/7/2008
5. E-mail communication.

Index